AREPA

AREPA

CLASSIC AND CONTEMPORARY RECIPES FOR VENEZUELA'S DAILY BREAD

IRENA STEIN

PHOTOGRAPHY BY IRENA STEIN

RYLAND PETERS & SMALL
LONDON • NEW YORK

"My faith in the potential of our white, round corn bread relies on its ability to make alliances with other foods and become a tasty, complete, fast and heterogenous food option. Perhaps the possibility of opening up to other flavours and other cultures is provided by the cosmopolitan spirit that distinguishes the Venezuelan cuisine, in which our arepa holds a place of honour."

Armando Scannone, Gastronome, Author of
Mi Cocina, a la manera de Caracas.

"For Venezuelans, it's kind of hard to talk about the arepa; it's pretty difficult, almost like talking about our own mother. You never know where to start with so many things to say and remember. Because the arepa, like our own mother, is always there for us. Our folklore says that every Venezuelan child is 'born with an arepa under their arm'. I think it's a beautiful affirmation about the happy existence that every person that comes to the world deserves."

Laureano Márquez, Journalist, Humorist, Actor, Writer. Caracas.

DEDICATION

Since 2013, approximately seven million Venezuelan citizens have left their land due to the circumstances in their home country. Now dispersed throughout the world, this book is dedicated to them.

Author: Irena Stein
Co-author and creator of arepa recipes: Eduardo Egui
Contributor and creator of appetizer and dessert recipes: David Zamudio, executive chef of Alma Cocina Latina, Baltimore
Designer: Geoff Borin
Creative director: Leslie Harrington
Editorial director: Julia Charles
Head of production: Patricia Harrington
Photographer and Food Stylist: Irena Stein
Props stylists: Annie Lampe and Irena Stein
Editor: Lisa Pendreigh
Proofreader: Jo Ireson
Indexer: Hilary Bird

First published in 2023 by Ryland Peters & Small
20–21 Jockey's Fields,   341 E 116th Street
London WC1R 4BW   New York NY 10029
www.rylandpeters.com

10 9 8 7 6 5 4 3 2 1

Text and photographs © Irena Stein 2023

Design © Ryland Peters & Small 2023

Map on pages 12–13 © Elisa Murillo

ISBN: 978-1-78879-517-3

Printed in China

RECIPE NOTES

• Metric, imperial and volumetric cup measurements are given for each recipe. Follow only one set of measurements throughout a recipe as they are not interchangeable.

• Cooking times given are for guidance only, as individual ovens vary. If using a convection (fan) oven, follow the manufacturer's instructions concerning oven temperatures.

• When deep-frying, heat the oil to the specified temperature, then slowly and carefully lower the food into the hot oil to avoid splashes. Wear long sleeves to protect your arms and never leave the pan unattended.

CONTENTS

INTRODUCTION TO THE AREPA

Round and pale, like a full moon, the arepa is a great Venezuelan treasure. For centuries it has been at the centre of the table in every home across this tropical region of the world, a region that, at the present time, includes all of Colombian and Venezuelan territories.

The arepa is loved by all for its deliciousness, its versatility and its easy preparation. It is loved so much that in Venezuela it is eaten at any time of the day – for breakfast, for lunch, for dinner. It is even enjoyed at 4am (the most 'democratic hour' of the day) when die-hard party animals, no matter what their social backgrounds, recover together from the excesses of a long night, in some 'arepera', they love.

Over the last decade, the destiny of this simple crispy corn patty has taken a turn. The arepa has crossed existing frontiers and travelled beyond the region to all corners of the world. As the difficult political and economic situations in Venezuela became increasingly unbearable, the number of Venezuelans emigrating began to rise. With each individual or family who left, so went a bag or two of Harina P.A.N., the pre-cooked white maize flour (cornmeal) used by almost all Venezuelans to make arepas.

Many of these émigré households, now established in countries around the globe, shared arepas with their new friends, wherever they went. Arepas have been so very enthusiastically received that, no matter what their original professions back home, Venezuelans opened arepa bars, restaurants and food trucks in every continent. Arepa fever has spread fast and Harina P.A.N. is now sold in over 90 countries.

Just as the taco became a worldwide phenomenon once Mexicans began to migrate in large numbers, successfully sharing their own daily bread, the arepa is now the popular new street food par excellence, receiving the same enthusiastic acceptance. A fast-growing number of food lovers are discovering Venezuela's national treasure, choosing to sate their hunger with easy, inexpensive, flavourful arepas with their almost infinite variety of fillings.

While living in the United States and observing the rapid growth in popularity of this corn patty internationally, I came to realize that its strength lies in the fact that it is extremely user-friendly: the neutral flavour of the basic arepa provides a versatile backdrop for any other ingredient, even those far removed from traditional Venezuelan flavours, perhaps even more so than the taco.

Naturally, all this sparked the idea of writing a book, describing the voyage of the arepa. During my research, I discovered that there were only a few short

publications dedicated to arepas or passing mentions of arepas in larger Latin American cookbooks. Once I knew how little the arepa was represented in literature, this project became more important as this book would turn out to be the first comprehensive arepa cookbook in the world.

As our conversations as immigrant cooks continued in our community of Baltimore, we shared our kitchen stories with colleagues. We began to think of the arepa as our very own cultural ambassador and as a symbol of friendship. Everyone loves arepas, so they are ideal for cultural liaison.

I have always believed that food can bring people together, promoting dialogue and peace in every community. What is better than sharing an arepa or two? What if this friendly arepa were dressed in foreign flavours? Thus was born the idea of adorning some of the arepas featured in this book with ingredients originating in different cultures. And it worked out very well. Any flavour does indeed marry well with this round crispy marvel.

This book is conceived as an invitation to place the arepa at the heart of your kitchen, as a form of travel and exploration. Friends and family will most happily join you at a table to eat them. Their versatility will also allow you to garnish them with whatever you choose, whatever leftovers are in your fridge. Arepas are an inexpensive delight loved by all.

Making this book has a profound meaning, as we take our arepas, our friendly 'daily bread', to tables in every corner of the world. Since many of you have never travelled to the tropical land of Venezuela, we have included images of its landscape and its people to set the scene as well as telling the story of the arepa.

Irena Stein
Baltimore, March 2023

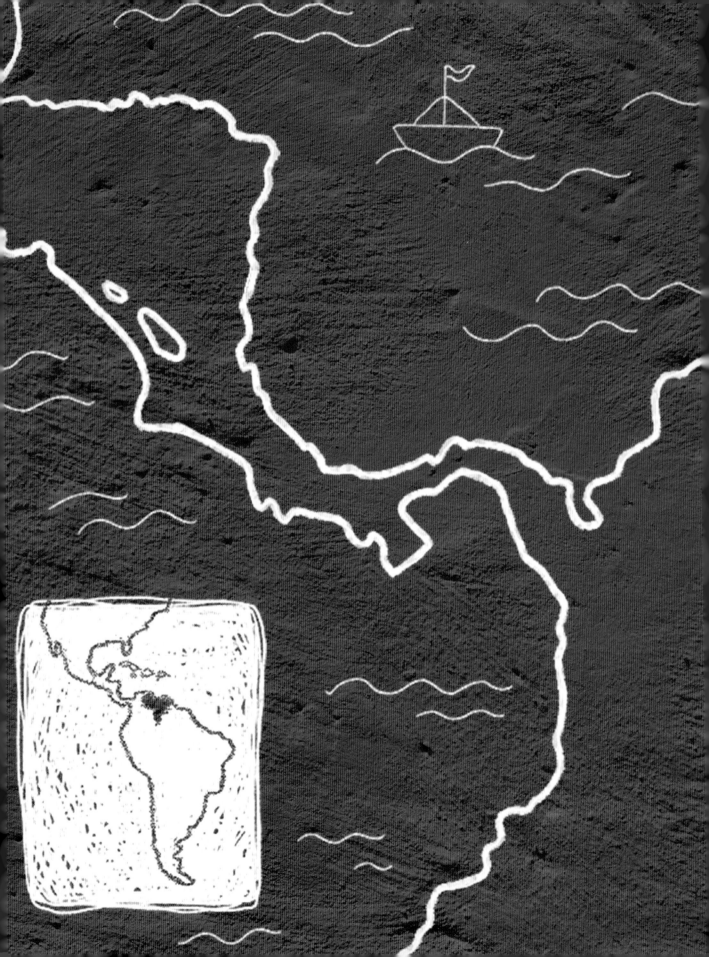

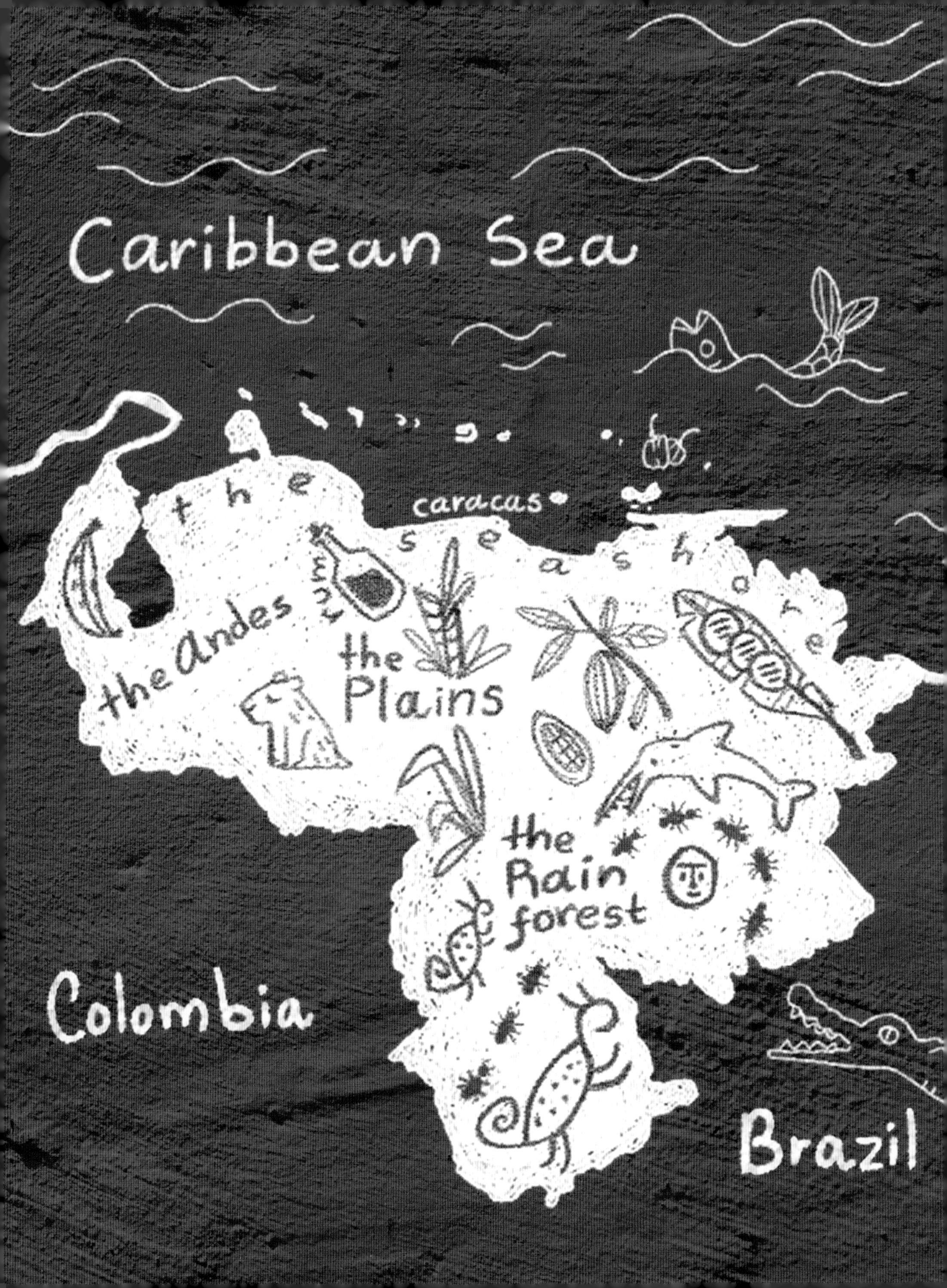
Caribbean Sea
caracas
the seashore
rum
the Andes
the Plains
the Rain forest
Colombia
Brazil

THE VENEZUELAN AREPA: BRIEF NOTES ABOUT ITS HISTORY

Venezuelan arepas can be found nowadays in a variety of gastronomic settings across the world and the locations to savour them seem to multiply with surprising vigour. The most powerful trait the arepa has is its distinctive neutrality, allowing it to accommodate dissimilar ingredients and flavours and turning it into a succulent experience.

The arepa, that round, white corn bread, has been present in the palate and collective memory of Venezuelans even before that territory had a name. Researchers have been able to trace the presence of these 'solar discs' to the dietary and nutrition habits of the indigenous population, centuries before Christopher Columbus arrived in this so-called 'Land of Grace'. Archeologists have found that while maize (corn) appeared into the territory now known as Venezuela somewhere around 1000 BC, their inhabitants were already grinding the grains with rocks and — with added water — making balls of dough they later squashed to give them a round shape and cook them on flat clay dishes called 'aripos' around 1000 AD. [1]

Familiar mostly to wheat, which was unavailable then in our continent, Spaniards soon learned about maize and began calling it 'Wheat of the Indies', among other things because this grain was used to make the indigenous bread. Faced with the need to substitute wheat and the difficulties to feed themselves, corn and arepas were gradually added to the diet of the Spanish settlers then.

Tools and techniques to make arepas also changed slowly. European settlers and African slaves used different methods and instruments for grinding the grain or preparing and cooking the dough arepas were made of. It was not unusual to find implements such as iron gridles (budares) and aripos or iron grinders and large, African-like wooden mortars and pestles (pilones), either coexisting or those new implements substituting the traditional ones.

As in most cultures, mostly all of food preparations and cooking routines have been performed by women and the old-fashioned way of making arepas was not the exception. The fast, accelerated pace of industrialization and modernization of the country during the second half of twentieth century completely altered family and societal dynamics; among the many changes induced by it, one that stands out was the growing number of women entering the work force — and consequently, causing a decline in their availability for meal preparation in the household. Other shifts in consumption patterns of the population would also de-emphasize the relevance of arepas as part of Venezuelans' staple diet.

The invention of pre-cooked maize flour was a lifesaver for this tradition that had spanned for centuries. In 1960, under the brand Harina P.A.N. (Producto Alimenticio Nacional) pioneered by Empresas Polar in Venezuela, this industrially manufactured product started to be distributed nationwide, and by making it available to the general market, consumption of arepas rose quickly, and some decades later it extended even beyond our borders to such an extent that, by 2022, Harina P.A.N. corn meal could be found in more than ninety countries across the globe. Iron grinders and *'pilones'* became a nostalgic expression of the milled corn arepa — as tasty as it is time-consuming to prepare — which was substituted for the arepa made with industrial maize flour, although in some inland regions of the country the preference for old-fashioned arepas is still alive.

Modernizing winds also brought changes in consumption patterns as well as the way arepas were eaten and enjoyed. Establishments called *'areperas'*, where arepas were made and stuffed quickly with a wide variety of ingredients, became quite popular in urban environments and blossomed in every city and town. The popularity, convenience and gastronomic possibilities of the stuffed arepa — also referred to as *'tostadas'* — made of our national bread a full meal, and all across the country, areperas gradually transitioned into restaurants where also typical Venezuelan food was commonly offered.

European immigrants, mostly of Spanish and Portuguese provenance, were quite entrepreneurlng in the food business and particularly, in the shaping and managing this type of establishments during the second half of last century. Starting relatively small and modest, these immigrants launched their areperas with fillings made of mostly local ingredients and preparations, but shortly thereafter they added new fillings with flavours that connected to their homeland tastes and uses. Along with pulled beef or telita cheese arepas, other fillings like pickled octopus or tuna, or Gouda cheese with Spanish chorizo, or meats and cold cuts, cheeses or stews became immediate favourites, making it all evident that arepas had a boundless potential for creating gastronomic and cultural dialogues with local and foreign foodstuffs alike.

During the last decade, we have witnessed how almost seven million Venezuelans have emigrated, hoping to find new, more promising opportunities abroad, and so has the stuffed arepa. With this diaspora, many Venezuelans found that arepas could be a marketable opportunity in their new destinations: they are easy to make and savour, fast and economical, and given their simplicity and versatility, they are always ready to connect with other food cultures. In fact, arepas have become a sort of culinary ambassador of Venezuela. After all, arepas are an expression, a language, and hence, also an opportunity to promote intercultural relations. This book is proof of it.

Ivanova Decán-Gambús
Caracas, January 2023

[1] Dorta Vargas, Manuel Felipe, *¡Viva la arepa! Sabor, memoria e imaginario social en Venezuela*. Editorial Alfa, Caracas 2015, pp. 15–16

AREPA: THE BASIC RECIPE

Receta de la arepa

Arepas are a cooked dough made of ground maize. They have been eaten in the northern region of South America since pre-Columbian times, most notably in Venezuela and Colombia, but they are also present in the cuisines of Bolivia, Panama and other Latin countries. Our arepas are made with the popular Harina P.A.N., the pre-cooked maize flour (cornmeal) that almost all Venezuelans use.

MAKES 6 AREPAS

720 ml (24 fl oz/3 cups) water, at room temperature

2 tbsp vegetable oil

2 tsp salt

a pinch of sugar (optional)

350 g (12 oz/2½ cups) Harina P.A.N. pre-cooked white maize flour (cornmeal)

In a large mixing bowl or bowl of an electric mixer, combine the water, oil, salt and sugar (if using). Slowly add the Harina P.A.N. pre-cooked maize flour (cornmeal) and mix the dough with your hands or electric mixer on medium speed for at least 10 minutes. The dough must be worked for a full 10 minutes to prevent the arepas from cracking when cooked. Once mixed, the dough should be free of lumps and soft to the touch.

Wet a paper towel or clean dish towel and wring out well. Cover the dough and let it sit for 10 minutes.

Preheat the oven to 230°C (450°F/Gas 8) and line a baking sheet with parchment paper.

Oil your hands. Pull off 170 g (6 oz) of dough and form it into a ball. Flatten the ball with your hands, pressing down to form an 11-cm (4-inch) disc that is 2.5 cm (1 inch) thick. Transfer the arepas to the prepared baking sheet and cover with the damp towel. Repeat with the rest of the dough to make 6 arepas, oiling your hands before forming each disc.

Heat a griddle pan over a medium heat and brush the pan with oil. Working in batches, put the arepas on the pan and cook for 5 minutes on each side or until lightly golden. Return the cooked arepas to the lined baking sheet.

Once griddled, put all the arepas directly on the rack of the hot oven. Bake the arepas for 20 minutes, flipping them after 10 minutes. The arepas are cooked when they have puffed up a bit, are brown in spots, and sound hollow when tapped.

Holding a hot arepa with a clean dish towel, cut three quarters of the way through using a serrated knife. Scoop out some of the soft insides to make room for the filling, leaving the crispy top of the arepa and a little of the soft inner. Add your choice of filling and serve immediately.

Notes: For best results it is essential to use Harina P.A.N. pre-cooked maize flour (cornmeal), which is made by cooking, drying and then grinding corn kernels. Each arepa recipe in this book has been tested using Harina P.A.N. and no other brand will yield the same results.

An arepa needs to be eaten as soon as it comes off the griddle, out of the oven or from the fryer. If you wait more than 15 minutes to serve an arepa once it has been cooked, its texture and taste is far less desirable.

To prep ahead, shape the dough and griddle the arepas. Leave to cool on a baking sheet. To chill, tightly wrap the entire baking sheet in clingfilm (plastic wrap) to prevent the arepas drying out. Store in the fridge for up to 2 days. To freeze, tightly wrap the griddled arepas in clingfilm (plastic wrap) with parchment paper between them to prevent sticking together. Store in the freezer in an airtight container.

When needed, thaw the arepas if frozen and bake in a hot oven as usual.

VARIATIONS ON THE AREPA

Variaciones de arepas

Plenty of fillings are best served in a plain arepa – one made with pre-cooked white maize flour (cornmeal) following our basic recipe on page 18 – but flavoured arepas can also be prepared by adding extra ingredients to the dough. Over the following pages you will find some alternative recipes for flavoured arepas, both savoury and sweet. You can follow any of our recipes or experiment with your own favourite flavours. Simply fold the additional ingredients into the plain arepa dough – try grated (shredded) carrots, chopped coriander (cilantro), chia seeds, or any other ingredient you can think of.

That said, a note of caution. Other arepa recipes suggest adding juice, such as carrot, beetroot (beet) or coriander (cilantro), to give the dough an intense colour. Adding liquid to the dough in this way may result in a mediocre arepa that is pasty, heavy and unpalatable.

FRIED GREEN PLANTAIN AREPA

Arepa de plátano verde

3 unripe green plantains
  (approx. 600 g/21 oz)

1 coriander (cilantro) root
  (approx. 15 g/½ oz)

20 g (¾ oz) sweet red pepper
  (*ají dulce*)

½ tsp lime juice

1 tsp salt

vegetable oil, for deep-frying

Peel and halve the plantains lengthways. Remove all the seeds (black dots) that run through the centre of each plantain.

Put the plantains, coriander (cilantro) root, sweet red pepper, lime juice and salt in a saucepan and cover with water.

Bring the water to a boil over a medium-high heat and cook the plantains until they are soft. Strain the plantains, discarding the coriander root and sweet red pepper but saving the cooking water.

While hot, mash the plantains to a smooth purée, then knead to make

sure there are no lumps. Leave to rest for 5 minutes.

Following the instructions on page 18, shape the dough into arepas. It will be sticky due to the starch in the plantains, so coat your hands in oil before handling the dough.

To cook the arepas, pour enough vegetable oil to cover the arepas into a large heavy-based pan, making sure it is no more than two-thirds full. Heat the oil to 190°C (375°F).

Carefully lower the arepas into the hot oil. Deep-fry the arepas for 4–5 minutes or until golden and crispy on the outside. Serve warm.

SWEET RED PEPPER AREPA

Arepa de ají dulce

MAKES 6 AREPAS

840 ml (28½ fl oz/3½ cups) water,
    at room temperature

¾ tsp salt

400 g (14 oz/2¾ cups) Harina P.A.N.
    pre-cooked white maize flour
    (cornmeal)

150 g (5 oz/¾ cup) sweet red pepper
    paste (ají dulce paste)

In a mixing bowl, combine the water and salt. Slowly add the pre-cooked maize flour (cornmeal) with one hand while simultaneously kneading the mixture with your other hand. Once mixed, the dough should be free of lumps and soft to the touch.

When everything is well mixed, add the sweet red pepper paste to the dough. Leave to rest for 5 minutes.

Following the instructions on page 18, shape the dough into arepas and cook on a griddle then in the oven.

BLACK PUDDING AREPA

Arepa de morcilla

MAKES 8 AREPAS

250 g (9 oz/1¼ cups) black pudding
(blood sausage)

720 ml (24 fl oz/3 cups) water,
at room temperature

1 tsp salt

500 g (1 lb 2 oz/3½ cups) Harina
P.A.N. pre-cooked white maize
flour (cornmeal)

vegetable oil, for deep-frying

Remove the casing from the black pudding (blood sausage). Heat a frying pan (skillet) over a medium heat and crumble in the black pudding. Cook until any excess fat has rendered. This is to prevent the arepa from cracking during frying.

In a mixing bowl, combine the water and salt. Slowly add the pre-cooked maize flour (cornmeal) with one hand while simultaneously kneading the mixture with your other hand. Once mixed, the dough should be free of lumps and soft to the touch. When everything is well mixed, add the cooked black pudding crumbs. Leave to rest for 5 minutes.

Following the instructions on page 18, shape the dough into arepas.

To cook the arepas, pour enough vegetable oil to cover the arepas into a large heavy-based pan, making sure it is no more than two-thirds full. Heat the oil to 190°C (375°F). Do not exceed this temperature as the arepas may burn.

Working in batches, carefully lower the arepas into the hot oil, avoiding any splashes. Deep-fry the arepas for 4–5 minutes or until golden and crispy on the outside. Remove the arepas from the pan with a slotted spoon and place them on a baking tray lined with paper towels to absorb any excess oil. Serve warm.

PORK CRACKLING AREPA

Arepa de chicharrón

MAKES 6 AREPAS

720 ml (24 fl oz/3 cups) water, at room temperature

1½ tbsp yellow pepper paste (*ají amarillo* paste)

1 tsp salt

350 g (12 oz/2½ cups) Harina P.A.N. pre-cooked white maize flour (cornmeal)

200 g (7 oz/1 cup) pork crackling or rinds (*chicharrón*), pre-prepared or homemade (see note)

vegetable oil, for deep-frying

TO SERVE

grated (shredded) white cheese

sour cream (*nata*)

In a mixing bowl, combine the water, yellow pepper paste and salt. Slowly add the pre-cooked maize flour (cornmeal) with one hand, while simultaneously kneading the mixture with your other hand. Once mixed, the dough should be free of lumps and soft to the touch.

Blitz the pork crackling or rinds to a fine powder in a food processor. Any large pieces will cause the arepa to crack as it is cooking.

Knead the pork crackling powder into the dough, removing any large pieces. Leave to rest for 5 minutes. Knead the dough again and then shape the arepas.

To cook the arepas, pour enough vegetable oil (or fat from the pork) to cover the arepas into a large heavy-based pan, making sure it is no more than two-thirds full. Heat the oil to 190°C (375°F). Do not exceed this temperature as the arepas may burn.

Working in batches, carefully lower the arepas into the hot oil, avoiding any splashes. Deep-fry the arepas for 4–5 minutes or until golden and crispy on the outside. Remove the arepas from the pan with a slotted spoon and place them on a baking tray lined with paper towels to absorb any excess oil.

Serve the arepas while still hot filled with grated (shredded) white cheese and sour cream (*nata*).

Note: You can use pre-prepared pork crackling or rinds (*chicharrón*) or make your own. Cut raw pork skin into bite-size strips. Melt some lard in a heavy-based saucepan over a medium heat. Add a bay leaf to the pan. Lower the strips of pork skin into the hot fat and cook, stirring regularly, for 30–40 minutes or until the skin is soft. Increase the heat to fry the strips until golden all over. Remove from the pan and drain in a colander. You will need double the weight of pork skin to yield the crackling needed.

COCONUT AREPA

Arepa de coco

Venezuelans generally make these arepas with yucca, but here they are made with a mix of pre-cooked white maize flour (cornmeal) and shredded fresh coconut. Other countries make similar fritters using different flours according to their culture: wheat, potato, malanga, cassava, pumpkin, rice, and more. They can be eaten as a bread with other dishes, such as the prawn curry on page 72.

MAKES 6 AREPAS

420 ml (14¼ fl oz/1¾ cups) water, at room temperature

120 ml (4 fl oz/½ cup) sugar cane syrup (see page 33)

1 tsp salt

280 g (10 oz/2 cups) Harina P.A.N. pre-cooked white maize flour (cornmeal)

50 g (1¾ oz/¾ cup) grated (shredded) fresh coconut

corn or vegetable oil, for deep-frying

To make the dough, combine the water, sugar cane syrup and salt. Slowly add the pre-cooked maize flour (cornmeal) and grated (shredded) coconut with one hand, while simultaneously kneading the mixture with your other hand. Once mixed, the dough should be smooth. Leave to rest for 10 minutes before shaping the dough into 6 arepas.

To cook the arepas, pour enough vegetable oil to cover the arepas into a large heavy-based pan, making sure it is no more than two-thirds full. Heat the oil to 160°C (320°F). Do not exceed this temperature as the arepas may burn.

Working in batches, carefully lower the arepas into the oil, avoiding any splashes. Deep-fry for 4–5 minutes, or until golden and crispy. Remove the arepas from the pan with a slotted spoon and place them on a baking tray lined with paper towels to absorb any excess oil.

Serve the arepas while still hot.

SWEET AREPAS WITH ANISE

Arepa dulce con anís

MAKES 10 AREPAS

720 ml (24 fl oz/3 cups) water, at room temperature

150 ml (5 fl oz/scant ⅔ cup) sugar cane syrup (see below)

15 g (½ oz/¼ cup) anise seeds

½ tbsp baking powder

¾ tsp salt

420 g (14¾ oz/3 cups) Harina P.A.N. pre-cooked white maize flour (cornmeal)

corn or vegetable oil, for deep-frying

FOR THE SUGAR CANE SYRUP (MELAO)

240 ml (8 fl oz/1 cup) water

175 g (1 lb 2 oz/2½ cups) unrefined raw cane sugar (such as *papelón*, *panela* or *piloncillo*)

To make the sugar cane syrup, heat the water and sugar together in a pan until the sugar dissolves and the mixture turns into a thin syrup. The syrup will thicken further as it cools, so remove the pan from the heat while the syrup still looks relatively thin (just as you would when making jam).

To make the dough, combine the water, sugar cane syrup, anise seeds, baking powder and salt in a mixing bowl. Slowly add the pre-cooked maize flour (cornmeal) with one hand, while simultaneously kneading the mixture with your other hand. Once mixed, the dough should be smooth. Leave to rest for 10 minutes.

Knead the dough and shape into balls. Cover each ball of dough with clingfilm (plastic wrap) or parchment paper, then flatten each one out with a rolling pin into a very thin disc, almost like a tortilla but not quite as thin.

To cook the arepas, pour enough oil to cover the arepas into a large, heavy-based pan, making sure it is no more than two-thirds full. Heat the oil to 190°C (375°F). Do not exceed this temperature as the arepas may burn.

Working in batches, carefully lower the arepas into the oil avoiding any splashes. Deep-fry for 4–5 minutes, or until the arepas bulge and turn crispy. Remove the arepas from the pan with a slotted spoon and place them on a baking tray lined with paper towels to absorb any excess oil.

Serve the arepas while still hot.

Note: Sweet arepas are not generally enjoyed as a dessert. Instead, they are eaten for breakfast with cheese as a contrast to their sweet flavour.

APPETIZERS
Entradas

REINA PEPIADA OR PABELLÓN CRIOLLO AREPITAS

Arepitas Reina Pepiada y de Pabellón Criollo

These arepa appetizers are simply a miniature version of the regular size versions of Reina Pepiada and Pabellón Criollo arepas found in later chapters of this book. Their small size makes them easy to eat.

MAKES 50 MINI AREPAS

FOR THE AREPITAS

1 quantity of basic arepa dough (see page 18) for each filling

FOR THE REINA PEPIADA AREPITAS

1 quantity of chicken reina (see page 152)

150 g (5 oz/ 1¾ cups) grated (shredded) yellow cheese

FOR THE PABELLÓN CRIOLLO AREPITAS

1 quantity of pulled beef (see page 139)

1 quantity of black beans (see page 86)

1 quantity of fried plantains (see page 50)

150 g (5 oz/ 1¾ cups) grated (shredded) white cheese

Prepare your filling of choice and set aside until ready to serve. As arepitas are so small, chop everything to a much smaller size than for a regular size arepa.

To shape the arepitas, pull off 20 g (¾ oz) of dough and form into a ball. Flatten the ball with your hands, pressing down to form a 4-cm (1½-inch) disc.

When making a large batch of arepitas, it is best to cover them so they do not dry out and crack. Place the arepitas on a lined baking sheet and cover with a damp cloth.

Preheat the oven to 230°C (450°F/ Gas 8). Heat a griddle pan over a medium heat and brush the pan with oil. Working in batches, put the arepitas on the pan and cook for 3 minutes on each side or until lightly golden. Return the cooked arepas to the lined baking sheet and bake in the hot oven for 10 minutes or until golden and crisp, flipping halfway through the cooking time.

Cut open the arepitas and scoop out a little of the soft dough inside. Fill the arepas, layering a little of each the different components, but without overfilling them.

BEEF TARTARE WITH CASABE
Tartar de carne con casabe

Here the beef tartare is accompanied by casabe flatbread. Casabe is made with yucca — an important ingredient in Venezuela that is used as widely as corn — so not only is it a great alternative to wheat bread, but it is also gluten free. You can, of course, use grilled flatbreads as an accompaniment instead, if you wish. Prepared in this way, the casabe can be used as a base for many appetizers or served as a side for dinner.

SERVES 4

FOR THE BEEF TARTARE

400 g (14 oz) beef tenderloin
salt and pepper, to taste

FOR THE DRESSING

25 g (1 oz) cornichons
20 g (¾ oz) red onion or shallots
4 tbsp finely chopped chives
75 g (2½ oz) aioli
1½ tbsp Dijon mustard
1½ tbsp gochujang (red chilli paste)
1½ tsp Worcestershire sauce
½ tsp granulated sugar
2 drops liquid smoke (optional)
a pinch of ground oregano

FOR THE CASABE

store-bought casabe flatbread
garlic and parsley butter (see page 162)

TO SERVE

extra virgin olive oil, for drizzling
freshly grated (shredded) Parmesan
kumache salt, to taste (optional)
lemon tree ants (or lemon zest)

Preheat the oven to 200°C (400°F/Gas 6).

To make the beef tartare, dice the beef into small pieces, but not so much that it turns into a paste. Do not grind the meat. Add salt and pepper to taste. Set aside.

To make the dressing, chop the cornichons and onion or shallots as small as possible. Combine with the remaining ingredients.

Mix the beef tartare with the dressing. Once the meat is fully dressed, let the beef marinate and the flavours mingle for 5 minutes.

Meanwhile, coat the casabe flatbread in the garlic and parsley butter, then toast in the hot oven for 5 minutes or until it turns darker in colour.

Alternatively, the casabe flatbread can be coated in onion ash. First, char an onion over an open flame until blackened all over. Meanwhile, toast the casabe flatbread in a hot oven for 5 minutes. Once the onion

is cool, put it in a blender and blitz to ash. Sprinkle the onion ash on top of the casabe flatbread.

Serve the beef tartare with the cassava and drizzled with extra virgin olive oil. Garnish the plate with a dusting of Parmesan, some kumache salt and lemon tree ants (or lemon zest).

Notes: Kumache salt and lemon tree ants are both rainforest ingredients. Although they are not widely available, except from specialist suppliers, we feel it is important to introduce them to as wide an audience as possible. Purchasing rainforest ingredients are a way of supporting the indigenous communities that are trying to find alternative sources of income to gold mining.

BUTTER LETTUCE SALAD WITH ORANGE AND THYME VINAIGRETTE

Ensalada con vinagreta de naranja con tomillo

The orange and thyme vinaigrette for this salad will surely become part of your repertoire of favourite dressings, and your friends will ask you for the recipe. Enjoy!

SERVES 4

FOR THE VINAIGRETTE

2 tbsp thyme leaves

400 ml (13 fl oz/1½ cups) fresh orange juice

30 g (1 oz) yellow pepper paste (*aji amarillo* paste)

3 tbsp honey

4 tsp Dijon mustard

80 ml (2½ oz/⅓ cup) Champagne vinegar or white wine vinegar

½ tsp adobo chilli paste

4 tbsp brown sugar

½ tsp ground coriander

1 tsp onion powder

300 ml (10 fl oz/1¼ cups) olive oil

FOR THE SALAD

2 little gem or butter lettuces

TO SERVE

pickled red onion, thinly sliced (see page 63)

jalapeño chillis or red bell pepper, de-seeded and finely sliced

avocado, thinly sliced

pine nuts

freshly grated (shredded) Parmesan

First, make the vinaigrette. Combine all the ingredients except the oil in a blender. Slowly add the oil in a trickle until it emulsifies. Set aside until ready to serve.

When ready to serve, cut the lettuce into wedges and toss in the vinaigrette until the leaves are fully coated. Transfer the dressed lettuce to a serving platter and garnish with the red onion, chilli or bell pepper, avocado and pine nuts. Finish the salad with some grated (shredded) Parmesan. Serve immediately.

BEACH-STYLE TOSTONES

Tostones playeros

Since they are vegan and gluten free, tostones are a crowdpleaser. They can be used as a base for appetizers, eaten as a snack or served as an accompaniment to many dishes, especially fried fish. The dressing for the coleslaw is a tropical version with mango and passion fruit purées. It is full of vibrant flavours.

SERVES 4–6

FOR THE TOSTONES (PATACONES)

2 unripe green plantains, peeled

vegetable oil, for frying

FOR THE MANGO COLESLAW

1 large white cabbage

1 mango, cut into fine matchsticks

1 bunch of coriander (cilantro), finely chopped

1 bunch of chives, finely chopped

FOR THE DRESSING

340 g (11½ oz/1 ¼ cup + 1 tbsp) passion fruit purée

170 g (6 oz/½ cup + 2 tbsp) mango purée

¼ tsp chilli lime powder

½ tbsp old bay powder

¼ tsp ground turmeric

¼ tsp ground coriander

2 tbsp sesame oil

1.2 kg (2 lb 10 oz/6 cups) mayonnaise

TO SERVE

avocado salsa (*guasacaca*, see page 164)

grated (shredded) Cotija cheese

To make the coleslaw, cut the cabbage into thin, evenly sized slices using a mandolin. Combine with all the other ingredients in a bowl. Set aside.

To make the dressing, place all the ingredients in a blender and blitz until smooth. Set aside.

To make the tostones, slice the plantain into thin rounds. Fry them in hot oil. Half way through, remove them from the oil and pound to flatten slightly. Return them to the fryer and continue to cook until golden. Place them on paper towels to absorb any excess oil. Set aside at room temperature.

When ready to serve, pour the dressing over the coleslaw and mix well until everything is fully coated. (Do not overdress the coleslaw as it can make the tostones soggy.)

Place the tostones on a platter. Add spoonfuls of the coleslaw on top of each tostone. Finish with a teaspoon of avocado salsa and a little grated (shredded) Cotija cheese.

SEA BASS CEVICHE

Vuelve a la vida

The name of this dish translates as 'Come Back to Life', but it is also often known as 'Break the Mattress'. Both names are good examples of Venezuelan humour, derived from the reputation shellfish enjoys as an aphrodisiac.

SERVES 4

FOR THE AREPITAS

1 quantity of basic arepa dough (see page 18)

FOR THE CEVICHE

2 good-quality medium sea bass fillets (or you can use dorado, escolar, halibut)

1 red onion, thinly sliced, for garnish

½ red bell pepper (or jalapeño, if you prefer it spicy), de-seeded and finely diced

salt, to taste

FOR THE VUELVE A LA VIDA SAUCE

1 heaping tbsp miso paste

270 g (10 oz/scant 1¼ cups) tomato ketchup

150 ml (5 fl oz/scant ⅔ cup) Worcestershire sauce

70 ml (2½ fl oz/generous ¼ cup) soy sauce

350 ml (12 fl oz/scant 1½ cups) fresh lemon juice

120 g (4 oz) rocoto chilli paste

40 g (1½ oz/1⅓ cups) coriander (cilantro)

3 garlic cloves

8-cm (3-inch) piece of root ginger

1 tsp sugar

TO SERVE

a handful of coriander (cilantro) leaves

2 limes, cut into wedges

Cut the fish fillet into small dice and place in a shallow, non-reactive airtight container. Cover the fish with ice cold water and 1 tablespoon of salt. Seal the container and refrigerate for 20 minutes.

Rub the sliced red onion with ½ tablespoon of salt.

Rinse the fish and the red onion slices under cold running water for 10–15 minutes.

Shape the arepa dough into mini arepitas and cook following the instructions on page 37.

To make the sauce, put all the ingredients in a blender and blitz until smooth.

Note: Instead of enjoying the ceviche with arepitas, you can serve it with green plantain chips, toasted cassava, choclo or boiled corn.

Del mar SEAFOOD AREPAS

AREPA WITH SWORDFISH GRAVLAX, PICKLED QUAILS' EGGS AND AVOCADO TARTARE

Arepa de pez espada, huevos de codorniz encurtido, tartar de aguacate

SERVES 6

FOR THE AREPAS

1 quantity of basic arepa dough
 (see page 18)

FOR THE SWORDFISH GRAVLAX

450 g (1 lb) swordfish loin, cleaned
 and skinned

500 g (1 lb 2 oz/2 cups) coarse salt

500 g (1 lb 2 oz/2½ cups) granulated
 sugar

2 tbsp grated (shredded) orange zest

1 tbsp grated (shredded) lemon zest

2 tbsp finely chopped dill

FOR THE PICKLED QUAILS' EGGS

18 quails' eggs

75 g (2½ oz) beetroot (beets)

75 ml (2½ fl oz/⅓ cup) pickling brine
 (see below)

FOR THE PICKLING BRINE

240 ml (8 fl oz/1 cup) white vinegar

1½ tsp salt

120 ml (4 fl oz/½ cup) water

1 tsp whole black peppercorns

125 g (4½ oz/2½ cups) chopped
 white onion

2 garlic cloves

2–3 bay leaves

1½ tsp pepperoncini

75 g (2½ oz/⅓ cup) granulated sugar

3 tbsp light brown sugar

2 tbsp mustard seeds

FOR THE AVOCADO TARTARE

140 g (5 oz/1 cup) finely diced
 avocado

25 g (1 oz/½ cup) finely diced red
 onion

1 tbsp finely chopped coriander
 (cilantro) leaves

1 tbsp olive oil

1 tbsp fresh lime juice

1 tsp Tabasco sauce

¼ tsp fine salt

Notes: You can buy good-quality smoked swordfish or salmon for this recipe, however, you can easily make the gravlax at home using wood chips, a kitchen blowtorch and a perforated tray.

The gravlax and quails' eggs both need to be made 48 hours ahead, so plan accordingly.

Two days ahead, make the gravlax. Place the swordfish in a non-reactive colander. Mix all the other gravlax ingredients in a mixing bowl, then cover the fish with the salt mixture. Press down firmly, making sure the entire fish is covered. Place the colander on a baking tray, then cover the fish with another pan to weigh it down. Leave the fish to dehydrate in the fridge for 2 days, discarding any liquid released every 6 hours.

Two days ahead, pickle the quails' eggs. Put the eggs in a pan, cover with water and bring to a boil. Once boiling, cover the pan and remove from the heat. Leave the eggs in the hot water for 12 minutes, then drain. Peel the eggs and set aside.

To make the pickling brine, put all the ingredients in a pan and bring to a boil. Once the sugar has dissolved, remove the pan from the heat and leave to cool.

Blitz the beetroot (beets) in a blender until smooth. Add the beetroot purée to the pan with the pickling brine and bring to a boil. Remove the pan from the heat.

Place the peeled quails' eggs in a heatproof glass bowl and pour over the pickling brine. Chill in the fridge for 48 hours.

To smoke the swordfish, rinse the fish in cold water and pat dry with paper towels. Lay it in a perforated tray and cover. Place the wood chips in a heatproof bowl and ignite them with a kitchen blowtorch. Place the perforated tray over the smoking wood chips and leave for 10 minutes. Once smoked, chill the

swordfish gravlax in the fridge until firm enough to slice very thinly.

To make the avocado tartare, combine the diced avocado, red onion and coriander (cilantro) in a bowl. Add the olive oil, lime juice, Tabasco and salt and set aside.

Following the instructions on page 18, shape the dough into 6 arepas and cook them just before serving.

Split open the arepas and remove some of their soft insides to make room for the filling. Slice the

swordfish gravlax as thinly as possible and lay on the bottom half of each arepa. Cut the pickled quails' eggs in half and nestle them on top of the swordfish. Finally, fill each arepa with spoonfuls of the avocado tartare.

FRIED GREEN PLANTAIN AREPA WITH PRAWNS AND AVOCADO

Reina de langostinos con arepa frita de plátano verde

SERVES 6

FOR THE AREPAS

1 quantity of green plantain arepa dough (see page 25)

FOR THE PRAWN REINA

18–24 king prawns (jumbo shrimp), de-veined, blanched in boiling water and chopped into large pieces

150 g (5 oz/1 cup) finely diced avocado

3 tbsp finely diced red bell pepper

3 tbsp finely diced red onion

a small bunch of coriander (cilantro), chopped

5 tbsp avocado mayonnaise (see page 152)

2 tsp salt

1 tsp Tabasco chipotle pepper sauce

TO SERVE

1 avocado, sliced

a handful of coriander microgreens (cilantro sprouts)

To make the prawn reina, combine all the ingredients in a bowl and mix well.

Following the instructions on page 25, shape the dough into 6 arepas and cook them just before serving.

Split open the arepas and remove some of their soft insides to make room for the filling. Lay the avocado slices on the bottom half of each arepa then fill with spoonfuls of the prawn reina. Finally, garnish with the microgreens (sprouts).

FRIED AREPA WITH FISH STEW, PLANTAIN AND PARMESAN

Arepa frita con huequitos, pescado, tajadas, parmesano

When shaping the dough, make small holes in the arepa – this speeds up the cooking process and makes it deliciously crunchy. Some people make only one or two holes, but you can make up to five.

SERVES 6

FOR THE FRIED AREPAS

960 ml (32½ fl oz/4 cups) water, at room temperature

1 tsp salt

450 g (1 lb/3¾ cups) Harina P.A.N. pre-cooked white maize flour (cornmeal)

FOR THE FISH STEW

500 g (1 lb 2 oz) cooked dogfish

5 tbsp annatto oil

200 g (7 oz/3¾ cups) finely diced white onion

4 tbsp finely chopped garlic

180 g (6½ oz/1¼ cups) finely diced red bell pepper

1 whole coriander (cilantro) root

2 tbsp ground annatto

2½ tsp salt

30 g (1 oz/⅔ cup) finely chopped coriander (cilantro) leaves

FOR THE FRIED PLANTAIN (TAJADAS)

2 ripe plantains (black on the outside)

vegetable oil, for deep-frying

TO SERVE

freshly grated (shredded) Parmesan

To make the fish stew, shred the cooked dogfish into small pieces. Heat the annatto oil in a saucepan and add the onion, garlic and bell pepper. Cook over a medium heat until the onion is translucent.

Add the shredded fish, coriander (cilantro) root and ground annatto to the pan. Cook over a medium heat, stirring regularly, until the fish stew has reduced by at least half.

Meanwhile, make the arepa dough. Combine the water and salt in a large mixing bowl. Slowly add the pre-cooked maize flour (cornmeal) with one hand, while using the other hand to knead the dough. Once mixed, the dough should be free of lumps and soft to the touch. Leave to rest for 10 minutes.

Next, fry the plantain. Peel and cut the plantain into thin slices on the diagonal, as if slicing a baguette. Heat the oil to 175°C (350°F) in a heavy-based pan, making sure it is no more than two-thirds full.

Working in batches, deep-fry the plantain for 2–3 minutes or until golden and caramelized. Remove the slices from the pan with a slotted spoon and place them on a tray lined with paper towels to absorb any excess oil.

Following the instructions on page 18, shape the dough into 6 arepas. Using your fingers, poke two holes in each arepa, making sure they go all the way through. Deep-fry the arepas in vegetable oil at 190°C (375°F) for 3–5 minutes until golden and crispy.

Season the stew with salt, remove the coriander root and scatter over the sliced coriander leaves.

Split open the arepas and remove some of their soft insides to make room for the filling. Lay the plantain slices on the bottom half of each arepa then fill with spoonfuls of the fish stew. Finally, grate over some Parmesan.

GRILLED SEAFOOD AREPA WITH GREEN PICADA

Arepa de parrilla de mariscos con picada verde

SERVES 6

FOR THE AREPAS

1 quantity of basic arepa dough (see page 18)

FOR THE GRILLED SEAFOOD

800 g (1 lb 12 oz) mixed seafood (we use 200 g (7 oz) each of octopus, small squid, large prawns (shrimp) and scallops)

4 tbsp olive oil

salt and pepper, to taste

FOR THE GREEN PICADA

100 g (3½ oz/2 cups) chopped coriander (cilantro)

100 g (3½ oz/2 cups) chopped parsley

7 garlic cloves

4 tbsp vegetable oil

1 tsp grated (shredded) lime zest

½ tsp sweet paprika

½ tsp fermented prawn (shrimp) paste

TO SERVE

confit bell peppers (see page 77)

rocket (arugula) leaves

spicy whey sauce (*suero picante*, see page 164)

First, make the green picada. Place all the ingredients in a blender and blitz for 4–5 minutes to make a smooth pesto-like sauce. Set aside.

Following the instructions on page 18, shape the dough into 6 arepas and cook them just before serving.

Toss the seafood in the olive oil and season with salt and pepper. Cook the seafood on a hot grill, taking care not to overcook them. Transfer the grilled seafood to a bowl and stir through a generous tablespoon of green picada to combine.

Split open the arepas and remove some of their soft insides to make room for the filling. Fill each arepa with a generous serving of the hot grilled seafood and top with some strips of confit bell peppers and a handful of rocket (arugula) leaves. Serve the remaining green picada on the side along with the spicy whey sauce, both of which can be added to each bite of the arepa.

Note: You can use whatever seafood or shellfish you prefer. We prefer a mixture of octopus, squid, prawns (shrimp) and scallops as they are all easy to grill.

Octopus can be bought already cooked or you can prepare it yourself. In either case, the best part of the octopus to use for this dish is the tentacles. They have a good percentage of fat that means they brown evenly on the grill.

PICKLED OCTOPUS AND CLAM AREPA WITH HEART OF PALM SALSA

Arepa de escabeche de pulpo y almejas con pico de gallo de palmito

Eduardo Egui currently lives in Barcelona and several of his recipes reflect the Mediterranean environment, especially the ocean and all its edible treasures.

SERVES 6

FOR THE AREPAS

1 quantity of basic arepa dough (see page 18)

FOR THE PICKLED OCTOPUS

240 ml (8 fl oz/1 cup) olive oil

4 tbsp white wine vinegar

30 g (1 oz/⅛ cup) thinly sliced onion

2 garlic cloves, thinly sliced

1 tbsp paprika

1 tsp pepper

300 g (10½ oz/1½ cups) cooked octopus

300 g (10½ oz/1½ cups) cooked clams (the cooking water can be used to make a sauce or to cook rice)

TO SERVE

heart of palm salsa (*pico de gallo palmito*, see page 164)

Two days ahead, make the pickled octopus. Heat the olive oil in a pan over a medium heat to 100°C (210°F). Add the vinegar, onion, garlic and spices.

Slice the cooked octopus into 2.5-cm (1-inch) pieces. Cut the cooked clams in half. Combine the octopus and clams in a bowl, pour over the pickling brine and mix well, cover and chill in the fridge.

When ready to serve, fully drain the pickled octopus and clams.

Following the instructions on page 18, shape the dough into 6 arepas and cook them just before serving.

Split open the arepas and remove some of their soft insides to make room for the filling. Place spoonfuls of the heart of palm salsa on the bottom half of each arepa and top with the pickled octopus and clams.

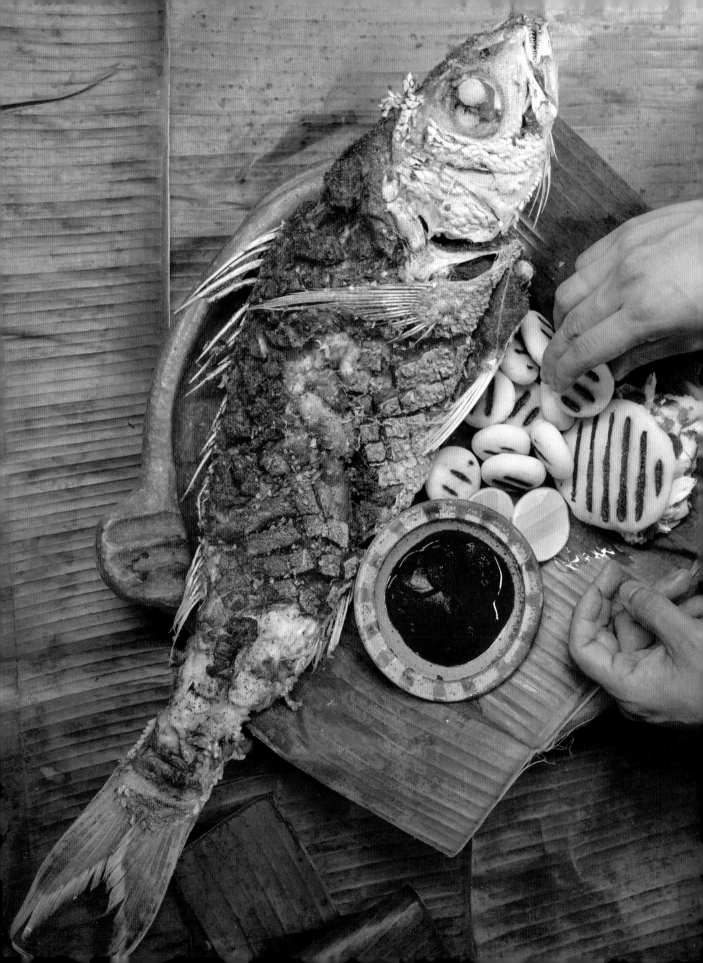

FRIED FISH AREPA WITH PICKLED BEETROOT

Arepa de pescado frito con remolacha encurtida y aguacate

Fried fish, or *pescado frito*, is the quintessential dish eaten on beaches along the Caribbean coast. It is usually served with slices of fried green plantain, known as *tostones*, coleslaw and cold beer, of course. Here we serve the fish alongside mini arepas.

SERVES 6

FOR THE AREPAS

1 quantity of basic arepa dough (see page 18)

FOR THE FRIED FISH

2.5 kg (5 lb 10 oz) red snapper (or other meaty white fish), cleaned

2 tbsp salt

vegetable oil, for frying

FOR THE MARINADE

50 g (1¾ oz/¼ cup) yellow pepper paste (*ají amarillo* paste)

4 tbsp grated (shredded) lime zest

300 ml (10 fl oz/1¼ cups) olive oil

20 g (¾ oz/⅔ cup) coriander (cilantro) leaves and stems

15 g (½ oz) spring onions (scallions)

FOR THE PICKLED BEETROOT

600 ml (20 fl oz/2½ cups) vinegar

200 ml (7 fl oz/scant 1 cup) water

200 g (7 oz/1 cup) chopped onion

125 g (4 oz/⅔ cups) granulated sugar

75 g (2½ oz/⅓ cup) brown sugar

3 garlic cloves

2–3 bay leaves

1 tbsp pepperoncini

3 tbsp mustard seeds

3 tbsp whole black peppercorns

½ tbsp salt

4 small raw beetroot (beets), peeled

TO SERVE

1 avocado, sliced

salt and pepper, to taste

Two days ahead, make the pickled beetroot (beets). Put all the ingredients except the beetroot in a pot and bring to a boil until the sugar has dissolved. Leave to cool.

Put the beetroot in a pan, cover with water and bring to a boil. Once boiling, cover and remove from the heat. Leave for 12 minutes.

Drain the beetroot and add to the brine. Chill in the fridge for 48 hours.

On the day of cooking, make the marinade for the fish. Put all the ingredients in a blender and blitz until smooth. Set aside.

Score the fish skin with a grid of incisions and sprinkle over the salt. Cover with the marinade and chill in the fridge for 2–3 hours.

Heat the vegetable oil to 190°C (375°F). Holding the tail, carefully lower the whole fish into the hot oil and hold it there for 1 minute before releasing the fish into the oil. Deep-fry the fish until the skin is crispy and the meat is soft.

Following the instructions on page 18, shape the dough into 6 arepas and cook them just before serving.

Split open the arepas and remove some of their soft insides to make room for the filling. Drain and slice the beetroot, then add slices of beetroot and avocado on the base. Fill with flakes of the fried fish. Alternatively, serve the fish with mini arepas to be eaten as a side.

Note: In Venezuela, we do not coat the fish in flour before frying, but you can if you prefer, in which case use wheat flour or rice flour.

GRILLED SARDINE AREPA WITH RED CABBAGE COLESLAW

Arepa de sardinas a la parrilla con ensalada rallada

I remember my first attempt at fishing. I was 5 years old and went with my two brothers to the beach where we sat on the dock to catch some sardines. The first thing I caught was my brother's nose. I will never forget those sardines. And his nose.

SERVES 6

FOR THE AREPAS

1 quantity of basic arepa dough
(see page 18)

FOR THE GRILLED SARDINES

1.2 kg (2 lb 10 oz) fresh sardines

120 ml (4 fl oz/½ cup) olive oil

1 tsp salt

FOR THE COLESLAW

120 g (4 oz) red cabbage

100 g (3½ oz) white cabbage

30 g (1 oz) carrots

20 g (¾ oz) red onion

50 g (1¾ oz/1 cup) chopped
coriander (cilantro) leaves

FOR THE DRESSING

500 g (1 lb 2 oz/2½ cups) mayonnaise

50 ml (1¾ fl oz/¼ cup) olive oil

3 tbsp apple cider vinegar

3 tbsp yellow mustard

2 tbsp fresh lime juice

5 garlic cloves

½ tsp Tabasco red pepper sauce

TO SERVE

2 limes, halved

island sauce (*mojo isleño*, see
page 164)

First, make the dressing for the coleslaw. Place all the ingredients in a blender and blitz until smooth.

To make the coleslaw, cut the vegetables into thin, evenly sized slices using a mandolin. Fill a large bowl with water and add the vinegar. Submerge the sliced cabbage in the water for 5 minutes, then drain well. Combine the sliced vegetables in a bowl and add 120 ml (4 fl oz/½ cup) of the dressing. Add the chopped coriander (cilantro), according to taste.

Following the instructions on page 18, shape the dough into 6 arepas and cook them just before serving.

Preheat a grill or barbecue to high. Mix the whole sardines, olive oil and salt in a bowl, making sure each fish is coated in oil. Place the sardines on the very hot grill and cook for 2 minutes on each side, or until golden all over. Once cooked, separate the sardine fillets from the bones using a small sharp knife. Squeeze lime juice over the sardine fillets as they come off the grill.

Split open the arepas and scoop out some of their soft insides to make room for the filling. Place a spoonful of the coleslaw on the bottom half, then add a layer of sardine fillets. Fill with more coleslaw and sardine fillets, as preferred. Serve with the lime halves for squeezing over.

Notes: The best way to cut the vegetables for the coleslaw is to use a mandolin as this will result in thin slices that are all even in size.

Any leftover dressing can be stored in a sealed jar in the fridge.

Instead of using whole sardines that need to be grilled or barbecued and then gutted after cooking, you can use pre-prepared sardine fillets that have been sautéed in a frying pan (skillet) for 1 minute on each side.

AREPA WITH CRAB SALAD, TOMATOES AND YOGURT SAUCE

Arepa de ensalada de cangrejo, tomate, salsa de yogurt

SERVES 6

FOR THE AREPAS

1 quantity of basic arepa dough (see page 18)

FOR THE CRAB SALAD

300 g (10½ oz/2 cups) fresh crab meat (do not use frozen)

80 g (2¾ oz/1 cup) finely diced red onion

60 g (2 oz/½ cup) finely diced celery

20 g (¾ oz/1 tbsp) finely diced sweet red bell pepper

2 tbsp finely chopped chives

2 tbsp mayonnaise

4 tbsp fresh lime juice

Tabasco red pepper sauce, to taste (optional)

FOR THE ROASTED TOMATOES

400 g (14 oz/2⅔ cups) cherry tomatoes

3 tbsp olive oil

2 tsp finely diced garlic

½ tsp sugar

1 tsp salt

a pinch of black pepper

FOR THE YOGURT SAUCE

240 g (8½ oz/1 cup) strained Greek yogurt

50 g (1¾ oz/¼ cup) coarsely grated (shredded) cucumber

30 g (1 oz/2 tbsp) finely diced white onion

1 tbsp olive oil

1 tbsp fresh lime juice

1 tbsp Sriracha hot sauce

1 tsp finely chopped dill

2 tsp salt

To make the roasted tomatoes, preheat the oven to 180°C (350°F/Gas 4). Halve the cherry tomatoes and mix them with all the other ingredients in a bowl. Spread the tomatoes over a baking sheet and roast in the hot oven until they start to dehydrate and turn golden around the edges. Remove from the oven and set aside.

To make the sauce, place the yogurt in a muslin cloth and squeeze out as much liquid as possible until it has the consistency of cream cheese. Place the grated (shredded) cucumber in a paper towel and squeeze out as much liquid as possible. Place the strained yogurt and cucumber in a bowl and mix together with all the remaining ingredients. Chill in the fridge until ready to serve.

Following the instructions on page 18, shape the dough into 6 arepas and cook them just before serving.

To make the salad, pat dry the crab meat with paper towels. Combine the crab meat with all the diced vegetables and herbs in a bowl. Add the mayonnaise and lime juice to taste. You can also add a couple of dashes of Tabasco red pepper sauce, if you prefer a little spice.

Split open the arepas and scoop out some of their soft insides to make room for the filling. Lay the roasted tomatoes on the bottom half, then add spoonfuls of the crab salad. Drizzle over the yogurt sauce. Serve with lime halves dusted with cayenne pepper for squeezing over.

FRIED SARDINE AREPA WITH PICKLED RED ONION

Arepa de sardinas fritas, con ensalada verde, gajos de lima y cebollas encurtidas

SERVES 6

FOR THE AREPAS

1 quantity of basic arepa dough
(see page 18)

FOR THE SARDINES

600 g (1 lb 5 oz) sardine fillets

1 tbsp olive oil

1 tbsp fresh lime juice

1 tbsp garlic powder

1 tsp chilli powder

300 g (10½ oz/2½ cups) plain
(all-purpose) flour

2 eggs, lightly beaten

240 ml (8 fl oz/1 cup) milk

300 g (10½ oz/5 cups) panko
breadcrumbs

vegetable oil, for deep-frying

lime segments, to serve

FOR THE PICKLED RED ONION

2 red onions, thinly sliced

1 tsp salt

juice of 2 lemons

4 tbsp apple cider vinegar

1 tbsp soy sauce

1 tsp ground coriander

1 tsp black pepper

FOR THE SALAD

30 g (1 oz) rocket (arugula) leaves

20 g (¾ oz) spring onions (scallions)

10 g (½ oz) coriander (cilantro) leaves

20 g (¾ oz) mint leaves

10 g (½ oz) white onion, thinly sliced

3 tbsp fresh lemon juice

2 tbsp olive oil

Following the instructions on page 18, shape the dough into 6 arepas and cook them just before serving.

To make the pickled red onion, put the sliced onion in a bowl with the salt and juice of 1 lemon. Leave to rest for 15 minutes. Cover the onion with water, swirl to remove the salt and then discard the water.

Pour in enough water to cover the onion, add the remaining lemon juice, vinegar, soy sauce and spices. Swirl to mix everything well. Cover and chill in the fridge for at least 6 hours or preferably overnight.

To prepare the salad, combine all the ingredients in a bowl and season with salt and pepper to taste. Set aside until ready to serve.

Marinate the sardine fillets in the olive oil, lime juice, garlic powder and chilli powder for 5 minutes.

To cook the sardine fillets, fill one bowl with flour seasoned with salt and pepper, fill a second bowl with the beaten eggs and milk, and a third bowl with the panko breadcrumbs. Individually coat each sardine fillet first in the seasoned flour, then in the egg mixture and lastly in the panko breadcrumbs.

Pour enough vegetable oil to cover the sardine fillets into a large heavy-based pan, making sure it is no more than two-thirds full. Heat the oil to 170°C (340°F).

Working in batches, carefully lower the sardine fillets into the hot oil, avoiding any splashes. Deep-fry the fillets for 4–5 minutes or until golden. Remove the fillets from the pan with a slotted spoon and place on a tray lined with paper towels to absorb any excess oil.

Split the arepas into two halves and serve them as tostadas, topped with the salad leaves, pickled red onions and fried sardine fillets. Finish with lime segments. Alternatively, split open the arepas, scoop out some of their soft insides to make room for the filling and fill with all the ingredients in the usual way.

AREPA WITH FRIED OCTOPUS AND MARINATED BELL PEPPERS

Arepa de pulpo frito y pimientos asados

SERVES 6

FOR THE AREPAS

1 quantity of basic arepa dough
(see page 18)

FOR THE OCTOPUS

600 g (1 lb 5 oz) cooked octopus
tentacles (see recipe)

100 g (3½ oz/¾ cup) plain
(all-purpose) flour

1 tsp salt

vegetable oil, for deep-frying

**FOR THE MARINATED
BELL PEPPERS**

300 g (10½ oz) red bell peppers

2 tbsp olive oil

1 tbsp balsamic vinegar

½ tsp fresh thyme leaves

½ tsp smoked paprika

½ tsp salt

Note: If you can find pre-cooked octopus, consider using it as an alternative to preparing your own. Octopus is tricky to cook well and can be rubbery when fried! If you do prepare your own, make sure you pat the raw octopus dry with paper towels to absorb all moisture.

Following the instructions on page 18, shape the dough into 6 arepas and cook them just before serving.

To prepare the marinated bell peppers, char the bell peppers directly over an open flame or under a grill until the skins are blistered and blackened on the outside.

Seal the charred peppers in a paper bag for 10 minutes. (The steam captured inside the bag makes the peppers easier to peel.) Using your fingers, peel the skin from each pepper, then slice them open, remove the seeds and cut into strips.

Combine the charred pepper strips with the remaining ingredients and chill in the fridge for 2 hours or until ready to serve.

To prepare the octopus, slice the tentacles into 2.5-cm (1-inch) pieces and place on paper towels to absorb any moisture.

To cook the octopus, sift together the flour and salt in a mixing bowl. Tip the octopus into the flour mixture and toss well, making sure each piece is fully coated. Shake to remove any excess flour and spread out across a tray.

Pour enough vegetable oil to cover the octopus into a large heavy-based pan, making sure it is no more than two-thirds full. Heat the oil to 160°C (320°F).

Carefully lower the floured octopus into the hot oil, avoiding any splashes. Working in batches, deep-fry the octopus, moving them in the oil with a slotted spoon to make sure they do not stick together, for 2–3 minutes or until golden and crispy. Transfer all the fried octopus pieces to a tray lined with paper towels to absorb any excess oil.

Split open the arepas and remove some of the soft insides to make room for the filling. Fill each arepa with the fried octopus, top with the marinated bell peppers and drizzle over the dressing.

AREPA WITH CRISPY OCTOPUS

Arepa de chicharrón de pulpo

SERVES 4

FOR THE AREPAS

1 quantity of basic arepa dough
(see page 18)

FOR THE OCTOPUS RINGS

600 g (1 lb 5 oz) cooked octopus
tentacles

1 tbsp yellow pepper paste
(*ají amarillo* paste)

½ tsp black pepper

100 g (3½ oz/¾ cup) plain
(all-purpose) flour

100 g (3½ oz/½ cup) potato starch

1 tsp salt

vegetable oil, for deep-frying

FOR THE SALAD

150 g (5 oz) cucumber

155 g (5½ oz) white onion

170 g (6 oz) spring onions (scallions)

FOR THE VINAIGRETTE

2 tbsp yellow pepper paste
(*ají amarillo* paste)

2 tbsp fresh lime juice

1½ tbsp white wine vinegar

1 tbsp salt

a pinch of black pepper

3 tbsp avocado oil

Note: If you can find pre-cooked octopus, consider using it as an alternative to preparing your own. Octopus is tricky to cook well and can be rubbery when fried! If you do prepare your own, make sure you pat the raw octopus dry with paper towels to absorb all moisture.

Following the instructions on page 18, shape the dough into 4 arepas and cook them just before serving.

To prepare the octopus, slice the tentacles into 2.5-cm (1-inch) thick rings and place on paper towels to absorb any moisture. Marinate the octopus rings in the yellow pepper paste and pepper. Chill in the fridge for 2 hours or until ready to cook.

For the vinaigrette, combine all the ingredients except the oil in a blender. Slowly add the oil in a trickle until it emulsifies. Set aside until ready to serve.

To prepare the salad, remove the seeds from the cucumber, but do not peel. Thinly slice the cucumber

and white onion using a mandolin. Thinly slice the spring onions (scallions) and place in a bowl of iced water to keep them crisp. Once all the vegetables are cut, combine them in a bowl and add a few tablespoons of the vinaigrette.

To cook the octopus, sift together the flour, potato starch and salt in a mixing bowl. Tip the octopus rings into the flour mixture and toss well, making sure each ring is fully coated. Shake to remove any excess flour and spread out across a tray.

Pour enough vegetable oil to cover the octopus rings into a large heavy-based pan, making sure it is no more than two-thirds full. Heat the oil to 160°C (320°F).

Carefully lower the floured octopus rings into the hot oil, avoiding any splashes. Working in batches, deep-fry the octopus rings, moving them in the oil with a slotted spoon to make sure they do not stick together, for 2–3 minutes or until golden and crispy. Transfer all the fried octopus rings to a tray lined with paper towels to absorb any excess oil.

Split open the arepas and remove some of the soft insides to make room for the filling. Fill with salad, then drizzle over the dressing and top with the fried octopus rings.

EGGS ROYALE AREPA

Arepa de salmón ahumado, salsa holandesa y huevos pochados

SERVES 4

FOR THE AREPAS

1 quantity of basic arepa dough
  (see page 18)

FOR THE HOLLANDAISE

120 ml (4 fl oz/½ cup) water

120 ml (4 fl oz/½ cup) white wine
  vinegar

4 tbsp chopped tarragon leaves

4 tsp black pepper

4 egg yolks

6 tbsp Dijon mustard

400 g (14 oz/5 cups) brown butter,
  melted

juice of 2 limes

FOR POACHED EGGS

8 eggs

3 tbsp white wine vinegar

salt, to taste

FOR THE SAUTÉED SPINACH

120 g (4¼ oz) spinach

20 g (¾ oz/1½ tbsp) butter

salt and pepper, to taste

TO SERVE

320 g (11¼ oz) smoked salmon

salt and pepper, to taste

To make the Hollandaise sauce, put the water, vinegar, tarragon and pepper in a small saucepan and bring to a boil. Cook until the liquid has reduced by half. Strain and cool.

Put the egg yolk, mustard and vinegar reduction in a heatproof bowl. Place this bowl over a bain marie on a high heat. Whisk continuously until the mixture has doubled in volume and has the texture of thick (heavy) cream. It is important to whisk continuously, but not necessary quickly.

While whisking, slowly pour in the browned butter. Add the lime juice and salt and pepper to taste. If necessary, adjust the consistency of the Hollandaise with a splash of water. Remove the bowl from the heat and set aside.

Following the instructions on page 18, shape the dough into 4 arepas and cook them just before serving.

To poach the eggs, fill a large saucepan with water and add the vinegar. Add the salt and bring to a boil over a medium heat.

Carefully crack an egg into a small bowl so the yolk does not break. Swirl the water in one direction and swiftly add the egg in a single motion. Repeat for a second egg. Poach the eggs for 3–4 minutes for a runny yolk or 4–5 minutes if you prefer a firmer yolk.

Remove the poached eggs from the water with a slotted spoon or skimmer and place in a bowl of warm water and set aside. Repeat for the rest of the eggs.

Meanwhile, sauté the spinach in the butter, making sure the leaves do not burn. Season with salt and pepper, to taste.

Split open the arepas and scoop out some of their soft insides. Use the arepas as a base for the rest of the ingredients. Place some of the sautéed spinach on each arepa, followed by the smoked salmon and finally a poached egg on top. Spoon over the Hollandaise sauce.

PRAWN CURRY WITH COCONUT AREPAS

Curry de langostinos con arepa de coco

Arepa meets India and creates an exquisite blend of flavours.

SERVES 4

FOR THE AREPAS

1 quantity of coconut arepa dough
(see page 30)

FOR THE PRAWN CURRY

1.2 kg (2 lb 10 oz) raw king prawns
(jumbo shrimp)

50 g (1¾ oz/¼ cup) curry paste
(see below or use shop-bought)

200 g (7 oz/2½ cups) red sofrito
(see page 159)

1.5 l (50 fl oz/6¼ cups) concentrated
chicken broth

1.3 l (44 fl oz/5½ cups) coconut milk

3 tbsp garam masala

80 g (2¾ oz/⅜ cup) granulated sugar

10 g (½ oz/¼ cup) chopped coriander
(cilantro)

3 tsp grated (shredded) lime zest

1 tbsp salt

1 tsp black pepper

FOR THE MARINADE

480 ml (16 fl oz/2 cups) vegetable oil

1 tbsp curry powder

1½ tbsp garlic paste

2 tbsp salt

1 tsp black pepper

½ tbsp ground turmeric

4 tbsp garam masala

FOR THE CURRY PASTE

2 tbsp vegetable oil

2 tbsp coconut oil

1 tbsp garlic paste

1½ tbsp root ginger paste

1½ tbsp lemongrass paste

2 tbsp curry powder

1 tbsp ground turmeric

1 tsp black pepper

240 ml (8 fl oz/1 cup) concentrated
chicken broth

TO SERVE

finely diced fresh coconut meat,
to garnish

edible flower petals, to garnish
(optional)

To make the marinade, simply combine all the ingredients in a blender and blitz to a paste.

Add the prawns (shrimp) to the marinade and chill in the fridge for 2 hours.

If making your own curry paste, warm the vegetable oil and coconut oil in a frying pan (skillet) over a medium heat. Add the garlic, ginger and lemongrass and cook over a low heat for 5 minutes. Add the spices and brown until it becomes

an aromatic paste. Next, add the broth and reduce for 10 minutes. Blend until smooth.

To make the curry, mix the curry paste and red sofrito in a frying pan. Add the concentrated chicken broth, coconut milk, garam masala and sugar. Lower the heat to medium and cook until you have a creamy consistency with the blended ingredients. For a sauce with an even smoother texture, blitz in a blender. Check the seasoning, then add salt and pepper to taste.

Following the instructions on page 30, shape the dough into 4 arepas and cook them just before serving.

Just before serving, add the marinated prawns to the curry sauce, cover and cook over a medium heat for 4 minutes. Spoon the curry into bowls, dividing the prawns equally. Scatter over the chopped coriander (cilantro), diced coconut and edible petals (if using). Serve with the coconut arepas.

Note: This marinade can be used with any type of protein that you prefer to use in the curry in the place of prawns.

FISH GOUJON AREPA WITH BALSAMIC TOMATO, BEETROOT AND AVOCADO SALAD

Arepa de pescado frito

FOR THE AREPAS

1 quantity of basic arepa dough (see page 18)

FOR THE FISH GOUJONS

360 g (12¾ oz) red snapper fillets (or other meaty white fish), de-boned

3 tbsp marinade (see below)

300 g (10½ oz/2½ cups) plain (all-purpose) flour

2 tsp salt

½ tsp black pepper

2 eggs, lightly beaten

240 ml (8 fl oz/1 cup) milk

300 g (10½ oz/5 cups) panko breadcrumbs

FOR THE MARINADE

120 ml (4 fl oz/½ cup) olive oil

50 g (1¾ oz/¼ cup) yellow pepper paste (*ají amarillo* paste)

1 tbsp root ginger paste

1 tbsp finely chopped spring onions (scallions)

1 tbsp grated (shredded) lime zest

2 tbsp finely chopped coriander (cilantro) leaves

FOR THE SALAD

100 g (3½ oz) avocado

50 g (1¾ oz) cooked beetroot (beets)

50 g (1¾ oz/⅓ cup) cherry tomatoes

50 ml (1¾ fl oz/¼ cup) balsamic vinaigrette (see below)

salt and pepper, to taste

FOR THE VINAIGRETTE

3 tbsp balsamic vinegar

1 tbsp Dijon mustard

100 ml (3½ fl oz/scant ½ cup) olive oil

First, make the marinade. Place all the ingredients in a blender and blitz until smooth.

For the fish goujons, cut the fish fillets into 5-cm (2-inch) long strips, cover them in the marinade and chill in the fridge for 2 hours.

For the vinaigrette, whisk together the vinegar and mustard. Slowly add the oil in a trickle until it emulsifies. Set aside until ready to serve.

Cut the avocado and beetroot (beets) into dice all the same size. Alternatively, use a Parisienne scoop or a melon baller. Cut the tomatoes into quarters and combine in a bowl.

Pour half of the vinaigrette over the salad in the bowl and toss until everything is fully dressed. Season with salt and pepper. Set aside.

Following the instructions on page 18, shape the dough into 6 arepas and cook them just before serving.

To cook the fish goujons, fill one bowl with flour seasoned with salt and pepper, fill a second bowl with the beaten eggs and milk, and a third bowl with the panko breadcrumbs. Remove the fish strips from the marinade and individually coat each one first in the seasoned flour, then in the egg mixture and lastly in the panko breadcrumbs.

Pour enough vegetable oil to cover the fish goujons into a large heavy-based pan, making sure it is no more than two-thirds full. Heat the oil to 170°C (340°F).

Carefully lower the goujons into the hot oil, avoiding any splashes. Working in batches, deep-fry the goujons for 4–5 minutes or until golden. Remove the goujons from the pan with a slotted spoon and place on a tray lined with paper towels to absorb any excess oil.

Split open the arepas and scoop out some of their soft insides to make room for the filling. Lay the goujons on the bottom half, add some of the salad and drizzle over more dressing.

SWEET RED PEPPER AREPA WITH BABY SQUID RINGS AND SQUID INK AIOLI

Arepa de ají dulce, ají dulce confitado, chipirones fritos, alioli de tinta de calamar

SERVES 6

FOR THE AREPAS

1 quantity of sweet red pepper arepa dough (see page 26)

FOR THE BABY SQUID RINGS

400 g (14 oz) baby squid or small squid (fresh or frozen)

2–3 tsp salt

3 tsp black pepper

50 g (1¾ oz/scant ½ cup) plain (all-purpose) flour (or rice flour to make it gluten free)

50 g (1¾ oz/¼ cup) potato starch

vegetable oil, for deep-frying

FOR THE SQUID INK AIOLI

400 g (14 oz/2 cups) mayonnaise

100 g (3½ oz/⅓ cup) garlic paste

2 tbsp squid ink

FOR THE CONFIT RED PEPPER

240 ml (8 fl oz/1 cup) olive oil

1 large sweet red bell pepper

TO SERVE

avocado butter (see page 162)

fresh lemon juice

Following the instructions on page 26, shape the dough into 6 arepas and cook them just before serving.

To make the confit red pepper, heat the olive oil in a pan over a medium heat. Add the sweet red bell pepper and cook for 20 minutes, or until soft. Remove the bell pepper from the oil, then peel away the skin and scoop out the seeds and ribs. Return the bell pepper to the oil and chill in the fridge until ready to serve.

To make the squid ink aioli, mix all the ingredients in a bowl and chill in the fridge until ready to serve.

Next, prepare the squid. Wash the squid under running water and remove the outer skin. Slice the squid into 1.5-cm (½-inch) thick rings and place on paper towels to absorb any moisture. Season the squid rings with the salt and pepper.

Sift together the flour and potato starch in a large mixing bowl. Tip the squid rings into the flour mixture and toss well, making sure each ring is fully coated. Shake to remove any excess flour and then spread the rings out across a tray.

Pour enough vegetable oil to cover the squid rings into a large heavy-based pan, making sure it is no more than two-thirds full. Heat the oil to 190°C (375°F).

Carefully lower the floured squid rings into the hot oil, avoiding any splashes. Working in batches, deep-fry the squid rings, moving them in the oil with a slotted spoon to make sure they do not stick together, for 2–3 minutes or until golden. Remove the squid rings from the pan with a slotted spoon and place them in a colander for a minute while you cook the next batch. Transfer all the fried squid rings to a tray lined with paper towels to absorb any excess oil.

Split the arepas into two halves and serve them as tostadas, spread with the avocado butter, topped with the confit red pepper and fried baby squid and finished with a squeeze of lemon juice. Serve the squid ink aioli on the side. Alternatively, split open the arepas, remove some of the soft insides and fill with all the ingredients in the usual way.

PASTELITOS
JUGOS
CAFE
EMPANADAS

VEGETARIAN AREPAS
Del campo

AN INTRODUCTION TO VENEZUELAN CHEESES

Acerca de los quesos Venezolanos

This book has an abundance of recipes that include cheese. That is because Venezuelans add cheese to almost everything! This tradition derives from the vast herds of cattle kept across the country, which arrived with the Spaniards when they colonized the country. From that point forward, Venezuelans started producing cheeses from unpasteurized milk.

The cheese arepa is the most popular type of arepa in the whole of Venezuela. We Venezuelans are brought up eating them. Children love these arepas, and often eat them in the morning before heading to school.

Any type of Venezuelan white cheese goes well with an arepa and its range of flavours suits all palates. When making this arepa, feel free to use any white cheese, such as queso fresco, queso Oaxaca, a cheddar of your choice, or a combination of cheeses.

Traditionally, a number of Venezuelan cheeses are made using animal rennett (cuajo rennet), but nowadays a number of producers are making cheese without rennet so that they are suitable for vegetarians. For those who are lactose intolerant or prefer to avoid mixing cheese with other animal proteins, you can omit the cheese from many recipes.

TO MAKE A CHEESE AREPA

Split open an arepa and scoop out some of the soft insides to make room for the filling. Spread both sides of the arepa with butter, then fill with grated (shredded) aged hard cheese (*queso de año*) and close the arepa.

AREPA WITH GOATS' CHEESE AND GRILLED VEGETABLES

Arepa de rulo de cabra y vegetales asados

SERVES 4

FOR THE AREPAS

1 quantity of basic arepa dough
   (see page 18)

FOR THE GREEN PICADA

30 g (1 oz/½ cup) chopped
   rosemary leaves

30 g (1 oz/½ cup) chopped
   thyme leaves

30 g (1 oz/⅔ cup) chopped chives

475 ml (16 fl oz/scant 2 cups) olive oil

1 tbsp salt

FOR THE GRILLED VEGETABLES

1 large onion

2 medium red or green bell peppers

1 small aubergine (eggplant)

1 medium courgette (zucchini)

2 tbsp olive oil, for grilling

TO SERVE

80 g (3 oz/⅓ cup) garlic and parsley
   butter (see page 162)

250 g (9 oz) goats' cheese
   (if possible, a 100% goats' milk
   cheese in a log with a diameter
   similar to the size of the arepas),
   thickly sliced

a handful of cress or sprouts

To make the green picada, put all the ingredients in a blender and blitz to a coarse paste. Check the seasoning and add more salt, if necessary. Set the picada aside until ready to assemble the arepas.

Following the instructions on page 18, shape the dough into 4 arepas and cook them just before serving.

Using heatproof tongs, hold the onion and bell peppers directly over an open flame to lightly char the skins all over and give the vegetables a smoky flavour. Do not allow the vegetables to turn white on the outside. If they do reach the point of whitening, the flesh will be burnt.

Once the onion and bell peppers are lightly charred, place the vegetables in a pan, cover with a lid and leave them to steam. This makes the skins easier to remove.

Wrap the charred onion in foil and cook in a 180°C (350°F/Gas 4) oven for 10 minutes, or until soft when pierced with a fork.

Remove the charred skins from the onion and bell peppers. Cut each vegetable into thin strips, then combine in a bowl and set aside.

Using a mandolin, cut the aubergine (eggplant) and courgette (zucchini) lengthways into very thin slices. Brush the slices with the olive oil and place them under a preheated hot grill (broiler) until caramelized on both sides.

When all the aubergine and courgette slices are grilled and you're ready to assemble the arepas, add the green picada to the bowl with the charred onion and bell pepper mixture.

Split open each arepa and scoop out some of their soft insides to make room for the filling. Spread both sides of the arepa with the garlic and parsley butter. Place thick slices of goats' cheese on the base of each arepa. Add slices of the grilled aubergine and courgette then the charred onion and bell pepper mixture. Top with a handful of cress or sprouts.

"If Christ's last supper had occurred in Venezuela instead of Jerusalem, he would have lifted an arepa instead of a slice of bread. Had this happened, what a delicious experience communion would be! What is important about this ritual is that both body and soul are fed."

Claudio Nazoa, Comedian, Cook and Writer. Caracas.

HUEVOS RANCHEROS AREPA WITH SPICY GREEN MOJO

Arepa de huevos rancheros y mojo verde

SERVES 4

FOR THE AREPAS

1 quantity of basic arepa dough
(see page 18)

FOR THE SPICY GREEN MOJO

30 g (1 oz/½ cup) chopped onion

80 g (3 oz/2 cups) chopped
coriander (cilantro)

20 g (¾ oz/½ cup) chopped parsley

1 tsp garlic powder

1 tsp salt

120 ml (4 fl oz/½ cup) white wine
vinegar

6 tbsp avocado oil

1 tbsp garlic paste

1 tsp pepperoncini (or other dried
chilli seeds)

**FOR THE HUEVOS
RANCHEROS SALSA**

80 g (3 oz/1¼ cups) red sofrito
(see page 159)

½ tsp pepperoncini (or other dried
chilli seeds)

¼ tsp ground cumin

1 tbsp white wine vinegar

225 g (8 oz/1 cup) good-quality
canned chopped tomatoes

½ tsp granulated sugar

1 tsp salt

TO SERVE

4 eggs

grated (shredded) white cheese or
braided cheese (optional)

2 large red bell peppers, charred and
peeled or from a jar

To make the spicy green mojo, put
all the ingredients in a blender and
blitz until smooth. Add more salt, if
necessary. Set the mojo aside until
ready to assemble the arepas.

To make the huevos rancheros salsa,
cook the sofrito and pepperoncini in
a frying pan (skillet) over a low heat
for 5 minutes. Add the ground
cumin and vinegar. Once the
vinegar has evaporated, add the
tomatoes, sugar and salt and cook
over a medium heat for 30 minutes.
Do not let the mixture dry out – if
necessary, add a splash of water.

Following the instructions on page
18, shape the dough into 4 arepas
and cook them just before serving.

Transfer the huevos rancheros salsa
to an earthenware dish or crockpot.
Crack the eggs on top then place
under a grill (broiler) for 2 minutes or
until the whites are cooked but the
yolks are runny. Once cooked, drizzle
over 2 tablespoons of the mojo.

Split open each arepa and scoop
out some of their soft insides to

make room for the filling. Lay strips
of bell pepper on the base of each
arepa, then spoon over some of the
huevos rancheros salsa with a
cooked egg. Finish with a spoonful
of the mojo. Alternatively, served
the arepas on the side and dip them
into the sauce and eggs.

AREPA WITH BLACK BEANS, FRIED PLANTAIN, AVOCADO AND CHEESE

Arepa de pabellón vegetariano

SERVES 4

FOR THE AREPAS

1 quantity of basic arepa dough (see page 18)

FOR THE BLACK BEANS

450 g (1 lb/2 cups) dried black beans, soaked overnight in 3 litres (3 quarts/12 cups) water

100 ml (3½ fl oz/scant ½ cup) concentrated vegetable stock (broth)

250 g (9 oz/1 cup) red sofrito (see page 159)

20 g (¾ oz/⅓ cup) fresh chopped coriander (cilantro)

1 tbsp sweet red pepper paste (*ají dulce* paste)

1 tbsp unrefined raw cane sugar (such as *papelón*, *panela* or *piloncillo*)

1 tbsp salt

150 g (5 oz/¾ cup) green picada (see page 82)

FOR THE FRIED PLANTAIN (TAJADAS)

1 ripe plantain (black on the outside)

1 litre (34 fl oz/4 cups) maize oil (corn oil), for deep-frying

TO SERVE

1 ripe avocado, sliced

30 g (1 oz/¼ cup) grated (shredded) white cheese

Drain the beans, discarding the soaking water, and transfer to a heavy-based pan or double-walled pot. Cover with fresh water and bring to a boil. Add all the other ingredients except the green picada to the pan. Cook over a medium heat for 3 hours or until the beans are soft, topping up the water as the beans cook. Once the beans are cooked, add more salt, if necessary, and the green picada. Cook for a further 20 minutes over a low heat.

Following the instructions on page 18, shape the dough into 4 arepas and cook them just before serving.

Peel the plantain and cut into thin slices on the diagonal, as if slicing a baguette. Heat the oil to 175°C (350°F) in a frying pan (skillet). Working in batches, carefully slide the plantain slices into the hot oil and fry for 2–3 minutes or until golden. Remove the slices from the pan with a slotted spoon and place on a tray lined with paper towels to absorb any excess oil.

Split open each arepa and scoop out some of their soft insides to make room for the filling. Lay slices of avocado on the base of each arepa. Place the fried plantain slices on top of the avocado, then fill the arepas with spoonfuls of the black beans. Finish with some grated (shredded) cheese.

DOMINO AREPA WITH BLACK BEANS AND WHITE CHEESE

Arepa dominó con caraotas y queso blanco duro

SERVES 4

FOR THE AREPAS

1 quantity of basic arepa dough
(see page 18)

FOR THE BLACK BEANS

450 g (1 lb/2 cups) dried black
beans, soaked overnight in
3 litres (3 quarts/12 cups) water

250 g (9 oz/1 cup) red sofrito
(see page 159)

1 tbsp salt

1 tbsp sweet red pepper paste
(*ají dulce* paste)

1 tbsp unrefined raw cane sugar (such
as *papelón, panela* or *piloncillo*)

100 ml (3½ fl oz/scant ½ cup)
concentrated vegetable stock
(broth)

20 g (¾ oz/⅓ cup) fresh chopped
coriander (cilantro)

hot sauce, to taste (optional)

TO SERVE

ripe plantain butter (see page 163,
optional)

30 g (1 oz/¼ cup) grated (shredded)
salty white cheese (such as *queso
llanero*) or braided cheese

heart of palm salsa (*pico de gallo
palmito*, see page 164, optional)

Drain the beans, discarding the soaking water, and transfer to a heavy-based pan or double-walled pot. Cover with fresh water and bring to a boil. Add all the other ingredients except the coriander (cilantro) and hot sauce to the pan. Cook over a medium heat for 3 hours or until the beans are soft and the broth is thick, topping up the water as the beans cook.

Following the instructions on page 18, shape the dough into 4 arepas and cook them just before serving.

Once the beans are cooked, check the seasoning and add more salt, if necessary, and the chopped coriander leaves. If you prefer a stronger taste, add the stems too. Add the hot sauce to the beans, if using, adjusting to taste.

Split open each arepa and scoop out some of their soft insides to make room for the filling. Spread both sides of the arepa with the plantain butter, if using. Add a spoonful of the black beans on the base of each arepa and finish with a handful of grated (shredded) cheese and the heart of palm salsa, if using.

Note: Any leftover black beans can be stored in an airtight container in the fridge or in individual portions in the freezer.

SWEET PLANTAIN AND CORNMEAL FRITTERS

Mandocas

We have included mandocas in this chapter, even though they are not actually arepas. These deep-fried fritters are traditional in the western state of Zulia. Zulians, who love plantains, created this dish by combining ripe plantain with pre-cooked maize flour (cornmeal) to make a dough. If you enjoy food that combines sweet and savoury ingredients, you will love these.

SERVES 4

FOR THE PLANTAIN PURÉE

2 ripe plantains, peeled, de-seeded and sliced

170 g (6 oz/¾ cup) unrefined raw cane sugar (such as *papelón*, *panela* or *piloncillo*)

1 tsp cloves

1 tsp anise seeds

FOR THE MANDOCA DOUGH

225 g (8 oz/1 cup) plantain purée (see above)

475 ml (16 fl oz/scant 2 cups) plantain cooking water

80 g (3 oz/⅔ cup) pre-cooked Harina P.A.N. maize flour (cornmeal)

1 tsp ground cinnamon

3 litres (3 quarts/12 cups) maize oil (corn oil), for deep-frying

TO SERVE

40 g (1½ oz/⅓ cup) grated (shredded) white cheese

sugar cane syrup (*melao de papelón*, see page 33)

Latin sour cream (*nata*)

To make the plantain purée, place the plantain slices in a large pan. Cover with water, add all the other ingredients and bring to a boil. Cook for 10 minutes until the plantain is tender, then drain and set aside the cooking water for making the dough. While still warm, purée the cooked plantain by mashing with a fork.

To make the dough, combine all the ingredients and knead well until it has the consistency of Play-Doh. If necessary, add some more of the plantain cooking water or maize flour (cornmeal) to achieve the correct consistency.

Divide the dough into 4 equal pieces and shape each one into a long rope. Bring the tips together to form a teardrop shape.

Pour enough oil to half-cover the mandocas into a large, heavy-based pan, making sure it is no more than two-thirds full and heat the oil to 185°C (365°F).

Working in batches, deep-fry the mandocas for 5–6 minutes or until crispy and golden. Remove from the pan with a slotted spoon and place on a tray lined with paper towels to absorb any excess oil.

Before serving, scatter over the grated (shredded) white cheese and drizzle with the sugar syrup to taste. Serve hot with the sour cream on the side.

FRIED EGG AREPA WITH SPICY MARINATED VEGETABLES AND AGED CHEESE

Arepa de huevos fritos, ensalada cruda picante, queso de año

It is best to use an aged hard white cheese that can be grated. However, if one is not available, you can use feta instead.

SERVES 4

FOR THE AREPAS

1 quantity of basic arepa dough
(see page 18)

FOR THE MARINATED VEGETABLES

150 ml (5 fl oz/scant ⅔ cup) olive oil

2 garlic cloves, thinly sliced

½ tsp pepperoncini

15 g (½ oz/⅛ cup) diced onion

15 g (½ oz/⅛ cup) diced sweet
red pepper

50 g (1¾ oz/⅓ cup) diced tomato

15 g (½ oz/⅛ cup) diced red
bell pepper

20 g (¾ oz/⅓ cup) finely chopped
coriander (cilantro) stems

100 ml (3½ fl oz/scant ½ cup) apple
cider vinegar

1 tbsp salt

TO SERVE

8 eggs (preferably free range)

olive oil, for shallow frying

40 g (1½ oz) grated (shredded) aged
hard white cheese

First, infuse the olive oil. Pour the oil into a saucepan, add the garlic and pepperoncini and warm over a medium heat. Cook for 30 seconds then remove the pan from heat. Leave the infused oil to cool slightly for 5 minutes.

While the oil is still warm, add the diced vegetables and chopped coriander (cilantro). Stir in the vinegar and salt, then set aside.

Following the instructions on page 18, shape the dough into 4 arepas and cook them just before serving.

To fry the eggs, heat some olive oil in a frying pan (skillet) over a medium heat. Break in the eggs and fry until the edges turn crispy, but avoid hardening the yolks.

Split open the arepas and scoop out some of their soft insides to make room for the filling. Place two fried eggs on the base of each arepa. Fill with the marinated vegetables and grated (shredded) cheese, then close the arepa.

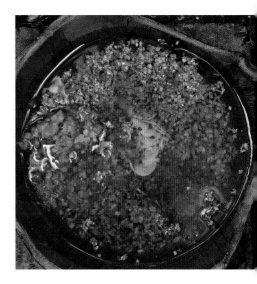

Alternatively, arrange the fried eggs and marinated vegetables on individual plates, scatter over the grated cheese and serve the arepas on the side.

AREPA WITH SPICED CARROTS, RED PEPPER CREAM AND PINE NUTS

Arepa de crema de pimentones asados, zanahorias glaseadas y piñones

SERVES 6

FOR THE AREPAS

1 quantity of basic arepa dough
 (see page 18)

FOR THE RED PEPPER CREAM

500 g (1 lb 2 oz) charred red bell
 peppers, peeled

10 g (½ oz/1 heaping tbsp) roasted
 pine nuts

3 tbsp olive oil

2 tbsp sherry vinegar

1 garlic clove

1 tbsp sweet Spanish paprika
 (*pimentón*)

½ tsp ground cumin

½ tsp cayenne pepper

1 tbsp salt

FOR THE CARROTS

80 g (3 oz/⅓ cup) citrus butter
 (see page 162) or coconut oil
 (if you prefer it to be vegan)

24 baby carrots, halved lengthways

3 tbsp rosemary honey or maple
 syrup (if you prefer it to be vegan)

1 tbsp harissa paste

1 tbsp ground cumin

2 tsp coarse sea salt

2 tsp freshly ground black pepper

TO SERVE

60 g (2 oz/¼ cup) citrus butter
 (see page 162, optional)

a handful of toasted pine nuts

a bunch of coriander (cilantro),
 leaves picked

150 g (5 oz) feta cheese (optional)

To make the red pepper cream, put all the ingredients into a blender and blitz until smooth. Chill in the fridge until ready to serve.

Following the instructions on page 18, shape the dough into 6 arepas and cook them just before serving.

Meanwhile, cook the baby carrots. Heat the citrus butter or coconut oil in a frying pan (skillet) over a medium heat. Add the carrots and cook them for 8 minutes or until al dente. Add all the other ingredients and cook for a further 3 minutes. Remove the pan from the heat and set aside.

Split open the arepas and scoop out some of their soft insides to make way for the filling. Spread the arepas with the citrus butter, if using. Lay the baby carrots over the base of each arepa, then add spoonfuls of the red pepper cream. Scatter over the toasted pine nuts and coriander leaves. Finish with some crumbled feta cheese, if using, then close the arepas.

AREPA WITH LABNEH AND CORN SALAD

Arepa con crema de yogurt y maíz

SERVES 6

FOR THE AREPAS

1 quantity of basic arepa dough
(see page 18)

FOR THE LABNEH

200 g (7 oz/¾ cup) Greek yogurt

2 tsp olive oil

2 tsp fresh lime juice

salt and pepper, to taste

FOR THE CORN SALAD

4 ears of corn, husks removed

30 g (1 oz/¼ cup) finely diced onion

20 g (¾ oz/⅛ cup) finely diced spring
onions (scallions)

30 g (1 oz/¼ cup) finely diced red or
green bell pepper

3 tbsp finely chopped mint

3 tbsp finely chopped parsley

FOR THE DRESSING

15 g (½ oz) chirel or jalapeño pepper,
de-seeded

1 tsp coriander seeds

½ tsp coarse sea salt

½ tsp freshly ground black pepper

3 tbsp extra virgin olive oil

2 tbsp lime juice

To make the labneh, put the yogurt in a muslin cloth and hang it over a bowl to drain. Mix the resulting labneh left in the muslin with the olive oil and lime juice. Season to taste.

Put the ears of corn in a large saucepan, cover with water, bring to a boil and cook until soft. To give the corn a smoky taste, place them under a hot grill (broiler) and cook for 10 minutes.

Cut the kernels of corn from the cobs. Place them in a bowl with the diced vegetables and chopped herbs.

To make the dressing, crush the chilli pepper to a paste in a mortar with the coriander seeds, salt and pepper. Add the olive oil and lime juice. Pour the dressing over the corn salad and toss to mix well.

Following the instructions on page 18, shape the dough into 6 arepas and cook them just before serving.

Split open the arepas and scoop out some of their soft insides to make room for the filling. Spread the arepas with the labneh, then add spoonfuls of the corn salad.

CLASSIC OMELET AREPA WITH GRILLED ASPARAGUS AND ARTICHOKE-TRUFFLE BUTTER

Arepa de omelette, alcachofas y espárragos

SERVES 6

FOR THE AREPAS

1 quantity of basic arepa dough
  (see page 18)

FOR THE ARTICHOKE-TRUFFLE BUTTER

6 artichokes

570 g (20 oz/2½ cups) unsalted
  butter

120 g (4 oz/1 cup) capers

1 tbsp truffle oil

1½ tsp salt

FOR THE GRILLED ASPARAGUS

12 asparagus spears

1 tsp olive oil

1 tsp salt

FOR THE OMELET

2 tbsp unsalted butter

3 eggs and 1 egg yolk, at room
  temperature

1 tsp salt

½ tsp black pepper

Clean the artichokes and reserve the hearts. Cover the hearts in salted water and cook for 8–10 minutes, or until they are easily pierced with a fork. Drain.

Melt the butter in a pan. Put the melted butter in a blender with the artichoke hearts, capers, truffle oil and salt and blitz well. Set aside.

Following the instructions on page 18, shape the dough into 6 arepas and cook them just before serving.

Trim away the fibrous ends of the asparagus spears. Heat the oil in a frying pan (skillet), add the spears and salt and cook for 1 minute. Add 2 tablespoons of water, cover with a lid and cook for a further 1 minute, or until the water evaporates. The asparagus should be al dente.

To make the omelet, melt the butter in a frying pan over a low-medium heat. Crack the eggs into a bowl and beat them vigorously until aerated and fluffy.

Pour the beaten eggs into the centre of the pan. With one hand, tilt the pan to move the egg mixture around the pan and with the other hand use a spatula to stir the eggs until they start to set on the bottom, but are still slightly raw on top.

Remove the pan from the heat, season the eggs with salt and pepper then quickly fold the sides of the omelet into the centre with the spatula. This ensures the edges finish cooking and seal the omelet, keeping the insides moist.

Split open the arepas and scoop out some of their soft insides to make room for the filling. Place spoonfuls of the artichoke-truffle butter on the base of each arepa. Cut the omelet into slices and divide them between the arepas. Finally, lay the asparagus spears, halved if necessary, over the omelet and close the arepas.

Note: To achieve the perfect omelet, always have all your cooking utensils to hand before beginning as the eggs cook quickly.

AREPA WITH BRIE, WALNUTS AND SWISS CHARD AND SPINACH SAUTÉED IN BROWN BUTTER

Arepa de queso Brie, mantequilla avellanada, espinacas y acelgas

SERVES 6

FOR THE AREPAS

1 quantity of basic arepa dough
(see page 18)

**FOR THE SAUTÉED
SWISS CHARD AND SPINACH**

30 g (1 oz) clarified butter

80 g (3 oz) Swiss chard

80 g (3 oz) spinach

salt and pepper, to taste

TO SERVE

320 g (11 oz) brie, at room
temperature (it best to use an
artisanal cheese with a rich flavour)

50 g (1¾ oz/½ cup) toasted shelled
walnuts

Following the instructions on page 18, shape the dough into 6 arepas and cook them just before serving.

To make the brown butter, put the butter in a saucepan over a very low heat and cook, stirring continuously, to avoid burning. (This allows the water in the butter to evaporate while the residual fat burns slightly, giving the butter a slight almondy aroma.) When the colour changes to light brown, remove the pan from the heat and set aside until required.

Quickly sauté the Swiss chard and spinach in the brown butter, but do not allow the leaves to burn. Let the sautéed greens drain briefly.

Split open the arepas and scoop out some of their soft insides to make room for the filling. Place slices of brie on the base of each warm arepa, so it slightly melts, then top with the warm sautéed greens.

"Some foods are merely just a desire, and here for the moment. The arepa was a necessity from the past, it is currently, and will be part of our forever future. Some food speaks to the soul in ways that words cannot. The arepa is one of them."

Kondwani Fidel, Poet, Writer. Baltimore.

CHEESE AREPA WITH SEASONAL SALAD VEGETABLES

Arepa de vegetales de temporada y queso cremoso de cabra

This arepa is an improvised seasonal recipe using ingredients at the peak of their flavour. For this salad, I slice the fresh vegetables as thinly as possible with a mandolin and serve them raw with a simple dressing that does not overpower the salad. Fill the arepa with your choice of cheese. In this case, I like a mild creamy cheese such as ricotta, mascarpone or creamy fresh goats' cheese.

SERVES 6

FOR THE AREPAS

1 quantity of basic arepa dough (see page 18)

TO SERVE

240 g (8 oz) selection of raw, seasonal salad vegetables, such as asparagus, carrots and courgettes (zucchini)

olive oil

fresh lime juice

salt and pepper, to taste

300 g (10½ oz) mild creamy cheese (such as goats' cheese or ricotta)

herbs and sprouts, to garnish

Using a mandolin, carefully slice the vegetables as thinly as possible. Dress the salad with the olive oil, lime juice, salt and pepper.

Split open the arepas and scoop out some of their soft insides to make room for the filling. Fill the arepas with the cheese and raw salad vegetables. Finish with fresh herbs and sprouts.

COCONUT FRITTERS

Buñuelos de coco

These simple fritters are called *buñuelos*. Countries across the region enjoy similar snacks made with different flours; here they are made with maize flour (cornmeal) but shredded fresh coconut is also incorporated into the dough. They can be eaten as a snack with coffee or as a dessert during a meal, dusted with sugar or topped with sugar cane syrup. To balance the sweetness of the syrup, at Alma Cocina Latina, we serve them with salty cheese scattered on top.

SERVES 6

FOR THE FRITTERS

1 quantity of coconut arepa dough (see page 30) made with sugar syrup with cloves (see below)

vegetable oil, for deep-frying

FOR THE SUGAR CANE SYRUP (MELAO DE PAPELÓN)

240 ml (8 fl oz/1 cup) water

175 g (6 oz/scant 1 cup) unrefined raw cane sugar (such as *papelón*, *panela* or *piloncillo*)

1 tsp cloves

TO SERVE

grated (shredded) salty white cheese

To make the sugar cane syrup, heat the water, sugar and cloves together in a pan until the mixture turns into a thin syrup. The syrup will thicken further as it cools, so remove the pan from the heat while the syrup still looks relatively thin (just as you would when making jam).

To make the coconut arepa dough, follow the instructions on page 30, but use sugar cane syrup with cloves, following the instructions given here.

Oil your hands. Pull off 10 g (⅓ oz) of dough and form it into a tight ball. Transfer the ball to a baking sheet and cover with a damp towel. Repeat with the rest of the dough.

Pour enough vegetable oil to cover the fritters into a large heavy-based pan, making sure it is no more than two-thirds full. Heat the oil to 160°C (320°F). Do not exceed this temperature as the fritters may burn.

Working in batches, carefully lower the fritters into the hot oil, avoiding any splashes. Deep-fry the fritters for 4–5 minutes or until golden and crispy. Remove the fritters from the pan with a slotted spoon and place on a tray lined with paper towels to absorb any excess oil. Serve hot with more of the sugar cane syrup and the grated (shredded) cheese.

MEAT AREPAS

De la tierra

A BRIEF HISTORY OF MEAT IN VENEZUELA

Breve historia de la carne en Venezuela

In his book *Nuestra Carne: Origen, cualidades y culinaria de la carne bovina venezolana*, Otto Gómez Pernía tells the story of our love for beef. The ranches across Venezuela were originally stocked with European cattle (*Bos taurus*), brought into the country by the Spaniards four centuries ago. Eventually these European cattle were cross-bred with the Zebu breed (*Bos indicus*), to make the herd better suited to a harsh tropical environment. The Zebu breed, most commonly Brahman in Venezuela, must make up at least 58% of the breed mix. This cross breeding is at the heart of our excellent meat.

Venezuelan beef is mostly free range and grass-fed. This makes for a leaner, tender, and healthier meat. The animals are slaughtered at a fairly young age, ideally under 30 months, to ensure the tenderness of the meat.

The traditional way to cook meat in Venezuela originated on the plains, located at the centre of the country. It is called *carne en vara*. Similar to a barbecue, the meat is cooked over a wood fire or coals, however, a piece of wood is inserted through the meat and it is rotated as it cooks.

FRIED BLACK PUDDING AREPA WITH REINA PEPIADA AND SWEET RED PEPPER PURÉE

Arepa frita de morcilla con Reina Pepiada

SERVES 6

FOR THE AREPAS

1 quantity of black pudding arepa
  dough (see page 28) made with
  1 tsp sweet red pepper paste

vegetable oil, for deep-frying

FOR THE REINA PEPIADA

1 quantity of chicken reina (see page
  152) made on the day of serving

TO SERVE

sweet red pepper and coriander
  (cilantro) purée (*chimichurri*, see
  page 164)

To make the black pudding arepa dough, follow the instructions on page 28 but add the sweet red pepper paste while kneading the dough. Shape the dough into 6 arepas and cook them just before serving.

To make the Reina Pepiada, follow the instructions on page 152. We prefer to use white breast meat that has been poached with aromatics such as onion, celery, carrot and coriander (cilantro) stalks. Once the chicken is cooked, shred the meat and allow it to cool before making the mixture.

To cook the arepas, pour enough oil to cover the arepas into a large, heavy-based pan, making sure it is no more than two-thirds full. Heat the oil to 190°C (375°F). Do not exceed this temperature as the arepas may burn.

Working in batches, carefully lower the arepas into the oil avoiding any splashes. Deep-fry for 4–5 minutes, or until crispy. Remove the arepas from the pan with a slotted spoon and place them on a baking tray lined with paper towels to absorb any excess oil. Leave the arepas to rest for 3 minutes before serving while still hot.

Split open the arepas and scoop out some of their soft insides to make room for the filling. Fill the arepas with the Reina Pepiada and top with spoonfuls of the sweet red pepper and coriander purée.

PORK CRACKLING AREPA WITH CONFIT IBERIAN PORK AND CATALAN ROASTED VEGETABLES

Arepa de chicharrón, cochinillo y escavilada Catalana

SERVES 6

FOR THE AREPAS

1 quantity of pork crackling arepa dough (see page 29)

vegetable oil, for deep-frying

FOR THE CONFIT IBERIAN PORK

800 g (1 lb 12 oz) suckling pig (use two hind legs, if possible)

1 tsp paprika

1 tsp onion powder

1 tsp salt

1 tsp black pepper

500 ml (17 fl oz/2 cups) olive oil

1 bay leaf

1 garlic bulb, cut in half

1 tsp black peppercorns

FOR THE ROASTED VEGETABLES (ESCAVILADA)

2 large onions

2 medium red or green bell peppers

2 medium aubergines (eggplant)

3 tbsp extra virgin olive oil

salt and pepper, to taste

Place the suckling pig in a heavy-based pan or double-walled pot and cover with the paprika, onion powder, salt and pepper. Leave to marinate for 2 hours.

Following the instructions on page 29, shape the dough into 6 arepas and cook them just before serving.

Once the suckling pig is marinated, add the oil to the pot along with the bay leaf, garlic and peppercorns. Cook for 4 hours over a very low heat. To confit properly, do not exceed a temperature of 90°C (200°F) while cooking the meat.

Once the suckling pig is cooked, remove from the pot and place on a baking sheet. Preheat the oven to 180°C (350°F/Gas 4). Roast the suckling pig in the hot oven until the skin is heavily cracked.

Meanwhile, using heatproof tongs, hold the onions, bell peppers and aubergines (eggplant) directly over an open flame to lightly char the skins all over and give the vegetables a smoky flavour. Do not allow the vegetables to turn white on the outside. If they do reach the point of whitening, the flesh will be burnt.

Once the onions, bell peppers and aubergines are lightly charred, place the vegetables in a pan, cover with a lid and leave them to steam. This makes the skins easier to remove.

Wrap the charred onions and aubergines in foil and cook in the 180°C (350°F/Gas 4) oven for 10 minutes, or until soft when pierced with a fork.

Remove the suckling pig from the oven and slice the meat with the skin on. Season to taste.

Remove the charred skins from the vegetable then cut into thin strips. Combine in a bowl and add the olive oil, salt, and pepper.

Following the instructions on page 29, deep-fry the arepas.

Split open the arepas and scoop out some of their soft insides to make room for the filling. Fill the arepas with the slices of meat and topped with a selection of roasted vegetables.

"Food is home. As an artist who has the luxury of visiting dozens of countries because of my work, I have to say that small restaurants in Baltimore have always brought me back home, constantly in fear of the dish not being there when I return. Arepas are home, and honestly I don't remember what I felt before experiencing an arepa and will not live a life without them."

D. Watkins, HBO Writer, *New York Times* Bestselling
Author of *Black Boy Smile*. Baltimore.

SMOKED PULLED PORK AREPA WITH BRAISED ONIONS AND MONTEREY JACK CHEESE

Arepa de pulled pork ahumado, cebollines a la parrilla, queso Monterey Jack

SERVES 6

FOR THE AREPAS

1 quantity of basic arepa dough
   (see page 18)

FOR THE PULLED PORK

200 ml (7 fl oz/scant 1 cup) olive oil

100 g (3½ oz/⅓ cup) garlic paste

50 g (1¾ oz/¼ cup) brown sugar

2 tbsp sweet smoked paprika

1 tbsp hot smoked paprika

2 tbsp onion powder

2 kg (4 lb 8 oz) pork shoulder

FOR THE BARBECUE SAUCE

200 g (7 oz/scant 1 cup) American
   yellow mustard

150 g (5 oz/scant ¾ cup) granulated
   sugar

150 g (5 oz/scant ¾ cup) brown sugar

200 ml (7 fl oz/scant 1 cup) apple
   cider vinegar

150 ml (5 fl oz/scant ⅔ cup) water

1 tbsp hot chilli powder

1 tbsp each black and white pepper

4 tsp cayenne pepper

40 g (1½ oz/½ cup) unsalted butter

4 tsp soy sauce

1 tsp liquid smoke (or chipotle chilli
   powder or smoked salt)

TO SERVE

1 white onion, grilled

1 avocado, peeled, pitted and sliced

240 g (8 oz/2 cups) grated
   (shredded) Monterey Jack cheese

A day ahead, prepare the pulled pork. Combine the oil, garlic paste, sugar and spices in a blender and blitz to a paste. Marinate the pork in this mixture for 12 hours or overnight.

The next day, preheat the oven to 120°C (250°F/Gas ½). Place the marinated pork in a roasting pan and cook in the hot oven for 6 hours.

Meanwhile, make the barbecue sauce. In a medium pot, mix all the ingredients except the cayenne pepper, butter, soy sauce and liquid smoke. Add the cayenne pepper and cook over a low heat for 20 minutes, stirring occasionally. Add the butter, soy sauce and liquid smoke and cook over a low heat for a further 10 minutes. Remove from the heat and leave to cool for 15 minutes before using.

Remove the pork from the oven and pull the meat into shreds using two forks. Add the juices from the bottom of the cooking pan and

400 g (14 oz/1½ cups) of the barbecue sauce. Set aside until ready to serve.

Following the instructions on page 18, shape the dough into 6 arepas and cook them just before serving.

For the grilled onion, using heatproof tongs, hold the onion directly over an open flame to lightly char the skin all over and give the vegetable a smoky flavour. Do not allow the onion to turn white on the outside. If it does reach the point of whitening, the flesh will be burnt.

Wrap the charred onion in foil and cook in a 180°C (350°F/Gas 4) oven for 10 minutes, or until soft when pierced with a fork. Remove the charred skin from the onion. Cut into thin strips and set aside.

Split open the arepas and scoop out some of their soft insides to make room for the filling. Lay avocado slices over the base of each arepa, fill the bottom half with pulled pork, then add grilled onions and top with grated (shredded) cheese.

Note: Any leftover barbecue sauce can be stored in an airtight container in the fridge.

AREPA SLIDERS WITH STEAK AND VEGETABLE CHIMICHURRI

Parrilla de chuletón de vaca con arepitas y contornos parrilleros

SERVES 4

FOR THE AREPAS

½ quantity of basic arepa dough (see page 18)

½ quantity of pork crackling arepa dough (see page 29)

vegetable oil, for deep-frying

FOR THE VEGETABLE CHIMICHURRI

½ tsp dried oregano

1 tsp pepperoncini

1½ tbsp warm water

100 g (3½ oz) red or yellow bell peppers

100 g (3½ oz) white onion

2 garlic cloves, finely chopped

30 g (1 oz/1 cup) finely chopped parsley leaves

1 tbsp white wine vinegar

TO SERVE

1 kg (2 lb 3 oz) aged T-bone, fore rib or rib-eye steak, about 5 cm (1 inch) thick and at room temperature

4 garlic chorizo sausages

400 g (16 oz) semi-hard white cheese

spring onions (scallions)

Following the instructions on pages 18 and 29, shape both doughs into mini arepitas and cook them just before serving.

Prepare the barbecue or grill at least 40 minutes before cooking.

For the chimichurri, rehydrate the dried oregano and pepperoncini in the warm water. Grill the peppers and onions on the barbecue, then dice and combine in a serving bowl. Add all the other ingredients. Set aside until ready to serve.

Place the steak on the grill and seal it on one side for 1 minute, then turn over to seal the other side. Season the steak generously with coarse salt and cook until it has an outer crust but is pink inside, or to your preference. Leave the steak to rest.

Meanwhile, cook the sausages on the grill for 12–15 minutes.

Cut the cheese into thick wedges and place in a griddle pan and cook on both sides.

Place the spring onions (scallions) on the barbecue or grill and cook until lightly charred.

Cut the steak lengthwise into 1-cm (½-inch) slices. Serve on a platter with the arepitas, grilled sausages, cheese and vegetables.

CREOLE PORK LEG AREPA WITH TOMATOES, AVOCADO AND VEGETABLE CHIMICHURRI

Arepa de pernil criollo, tomate, aguacate

SERVES 12

FOR THE AREPAS

2 quantities of basic arepa dough (see page 18)

FOR THE BRINE

800 ml (27 fl oz/3¼ cups) water

200 ml (7 fl oz/scant 1 cup) white wine

90 g (3 oz/¼ cup) fine salt

50 g (1¾ oz/¼ cup) sugar

5 garlic cloves

1 tsp thyme

2 bay leaves

FOR THE PORK

3 kg (6 lb 10 oz) pork leg

700 ml (24 fl oz/scant 3 cups) red wine

580 g (1 lb 4 oz/4 cups) roughly chopped carrots

1 kg (2 lb 4 oz/7 cups) roughly chopped onions

580 g (1 lb 4 oz/4 cups) roughly chopped green bell peppers

580 g (1 lb 4 oz/4 cups) roughly chopped celery

FOR THE TOMATOES

200 g (7 oz/1¼ cups) cherry tomatoes

2 tbsp olive oil

½ tsp salt

¼ tsp black pepper

½ tsp pepperoncini

1 garlic clove

TO SERVE

vegetable chimichurri (see page 121)

2 avocados, finely diced

A day ahead, brine the pork. Place all the ingredients in a bowl and mix until the sugar and salt are dissolved. Submerge the pork in the brine and set aside.

The next day, preheat the oven to 180°C (350°F/Gas 4). Remove the pork from the brine and put it in a deep roasting pan. Add all the remaining ingredients for the pork, cover the pan tightly with foil and cook for 3 hours (or 1 hour for each 1 kg/2 lb of pork). Baste the pork with the cooking juices in the pan every 30 minutes to create a caramelized crust on the meat.

When 40 minutes of cooking time remain, remove the foil so the outer layer of fat on the meat can brown and the flavours deepen.

To roast the tomatoes, cut them in half and combine in a bowl with the rest of the ingredients. Spread them over a tray and roast in the 180°C (350°F/Gas 4) oven for 40 minutes, or until they start to dehydrate and become golden around the edges. Remove from the oven and set aside.

Meanwhile, make the chimichurri following the instructions on page 121, but roasting the vegetables in the hot oven rather than grilling.

Following the instructions on page 18, shape the dough into 12 arepas and cook them just before serving.

Split open the arepas and scoop out some of their soft insides to make room for the filling. Slice the pork very thinly. Fill the arepas with the slices of pork and roasted tomatoes, then top with spoonfuls of the diced avocado and vegetable chimichurri.

Note: Pork leg is a very typical meal and a favourite of Venezuelans. It is customary to use the hind leg of the animal. Ideally it should be brined overnight before roasting, not only for a better taste but also for moisture, avoiding the dryness that often comes with cooking meat.

PABELLÓN AREPA

Arepa de Pabellón

SERVES 6

FOR THE AREPAS

1 quantity of basic arepa dough
   (see page 18)

TO SERVE

pulled beef (see page 139)

black beans (see page 86)

fried plantains (see page 50)

grated (shredded) white cheese

Make the basic arepas following the instructions on page 18. When ready to serve, split open the arepas and scoop out some of their soft insides to make room for the filling. Fill with the pulled beef and black beans, add a few fried plantain slices then top with grated (shredded) cheese.

The Pabellón Criollo is an iconic Venezuelan dish recognized as the country's national dish *par excellence*. Traditionally the Pabellón Criollo is made up of cooked white rice, black beans, shredded meat and slices of fried ripe plantain, served with cheese and avocado as accompaniments.

The Pabellón dates from colonial times, probably the eighteenth century. According to legend, it is essentially a collection of leftovers from the previous day's meal, made by the slaves of the haciendas, with only the plantain slices being freshly prepared specifically for the dish. There is another origin story that claims this dish is native to Venezuela's central west, because it is very common to see it on the menus of the gastronomic establishments there. It is also in this region where the ingredients of the Pabellón can be most easily obtained, because the Llanos, the Caribbean Sea, the Andes Mountains, Lake Maracaibo, and the Coastal Mountains have the most favourable climates of the entire nation for agriculture. Above all, it is the Creole culture that has had the greatest influence of all, leaving its mark on the vast majority of traditions throughout Venezuelan history.

When making this dish, keep in mind that you can use the leftovers of the shredded meat (*carne mechada*) and the black beans for a dinner, adding rice and fried plantains to it and omitting the arepa.

"The arepa is a symbol of Venezuelan food and when I eat one I get that taste from my country."

Leonor Giménez de Mendoza, Businesswoman and Philanthropist. New York.

FRIED PORK AREPA WITH KIMCHI

Arepa de cochino frito con kimchi

FOR THE AREPAS

1 quantity of basic arepa dough
   (see page 18) or pork crackling
   arepa dough (see page 29)

FOR THE FRIED PORK

1 kg (2 lb 4 oz) pork meat,
   50% pancetta and 50% shoulder

20 g (¾ oz/2 tbsp) garlic paste

2 tbsp vinegar

½ tsp ground turmeric

1 tbsp smoked paprika

½ tsp dried thyme

1½ tbsp salt

vegetable oil, for frying

FOR THE KIMCHI

1 Chinese cabbage

250 g (9 oz/scant 1 cup) coarse salt

2 litres (70 fl oz/8 cups) warm water

40 g (½ oz/scant ¼ cup) granulated
   sugar

2 tbsp soybean paste

4 garlic cloves

10-cm (4-inch) piece of root ginger

1 tbsp rice flour

2 tbsp fish sauce

1 tbsp chilli powder

3 tbsp sesame seeds

The kimchi needs to be made at least 8 days ahead in order to ferment, so plan accordingly.

There are different ways to make kimchi. You can separate the leaves from the stalk of the cabbage, then cut the leaves and stalk into large pieces. Alternatively, you can shred the cabbage. Feel free to use whatever method you prefer.

Make a brine by dissolving the salt in warm water. Submerge the cabbage in the brine and set aside for 12 hours.

Put all the other kimchi ingredients in a blender and blitz to a paste. Drain the brined cabbage, combine with the paste and mix well until the cabbage is completely coated.

Place the kimchi mixture in a sterilized glass container, seal with a tight-fitting lid and allow it to ferment in the fridge for at least 8 days, or until it reaches the preferred acidic, spicy taste. Remember to 'burp' the jar daily to release the gases that build up.

A day ahead, place the pork in a large pot with all the other ingredients except the vegetable oil and leave to marinate for 12 hours or overnight. When ready to cook the pork, pour enough water into the pot to cover the meat and cook over a medium heat until it starts to boil, then reduce the heat to low and cook for 1 hour. Remove the pork from the water to cool.

Once cool, fry the pork in plenty of vegetable oil heated to a high temperature (180°C/350°F), until golden. Strain the pork.

Following the instructions on page 18, shape the dough into 6 arepas and cook them just before serving.

Take the pork directly from the frying pan (skillet) and mix it with kimchi in a large bowl.

Split open the arepas and scoop out some of their soft insides to make room for the filling. Fill the arepas with the pork and kimchi mixture.

AREPAS WITH LAMB CUTLETS AND YOGURT AND MINT SAUCE

Arepa de cordero grillado, ensalada de aceitunas y salsa de yogurt y menta

SERVES 6–8

FOR THE AREPAS

1 quantity of basic arepa dough (see page 18)

FOR THE LAMB CUTLETS

1 kg (2 lb 4 oz) whole rack of lamb cutlets

1 tbsp coarse salt

1 tsp pepper

FOR THE GREEN PICADA

2 tbsp rosemary leaves

1 tbsp finely chopped thyme leaves

1 tbsp finely chopped mint leaves

120 ml (4 fl oz/½ cup) olive oil

FOR THE OLIVE AND ONION SALAD

30 g (1 oz/¼ cup) finely chopped pitted green olives

30 g (1 oz/¼ cup) finely chopped pitted Kalamata olives

100 g (3½ oz) tomatoes, skinned, de-seeded and finely diced.

50 g (1¾ oz) pickled onions

2 tbsp finely chopped mint leaves

1 tbsp fresh lime juice

1 tbsp olive oil

FOR THE YOGURT AND MINT SAUCE

220 g (8 oz) Greek yogurt

1 tbsp lime juice

2 tbsp finely chopped parsley leaves

2 tbsp finely chopped mint leaves

½ tsp olive oil

¼ tsp salt

¼ tsp pepper

First, make the green picada. Put all the ingredients in a blender and blitz until fully blended. Set aside.

An hour before cooking, marinate the rack of lamb cutlets in two-thirds of the green picada, salt and pepper at room temperature. (Bringing the lamb to room temperature before cooking is necessary for the meat to achieve the correct temperature.)

Grill the rack of lamb cutlets for 20 minutes for medium rare, or to your preference. Once the lamb is cooked, let it rest for 15 minutes.

Meanwhile, make the yogurt sauce. Put all the ingredients in a blender and blitz to a smooth, green sauce.

Following the instructions on page 18, shape the dough into 6 arepas and cook them just before serving.

To make the salad, combine the olives, tomatoes, pickled onions, mint leaves, lime juice and olive oil.

Once rested, slice the rack of lamb into individual cutlets, reserving any meat juices. Stir a generous tablespoon of the remaining green picada into the juices from the lamb. Pour these juices over the lamb cutlets before serving with the arepas, salad and sauce alongside.

Note: The picada is used as both a marinade for the lamb cutlets before cooking and as a flavour enhancer for the sauce made from the meat juices once the lamb cutlets are cooked.

BACON AND CHEDDAR AREPA WITH TRUFFLE BUTTER

Arepa de queso cheddar, bacon ahumado, mantequilla de trufas

SERVES 6

FOR THE AREPAS

1 quantity of basic arepa dough
  (see page 18)

FOR THE TRUFFLE BUTTER

280 g (10 oz/1¼ cups) unsalted
  butter

1 tbsp truffle oil

½ tsp salt

TO SERVE

300 g (10½ oz/2½ cups) grated
  (shredded) Montgomery cheddar
  (or other good-quality aged
  cheddar)

12 rashers (slices) smoked back
  bacon, fried to your liking.

Melt the butter, add the truffle oil
and salt and mix well. Before
refrigerating, cover tightly in cling
film (plastic wrap) to preserve the
truffle aroma.

Make the basic arepas following
the instructions on page 18.
When ready to serve, split open the
arepas and scoop out some of their
soft insides to make room for the
filling. Spread the arepas with the
truffle butter, then fill with the
grated (shredded) cheese and
rashers (slices) of fried bacon.

MONTGOMERY CHEDDAR

The Montgomery Family has
been making their world-famous
Cadbury Cheddar for three
generations, maintaining the
highest standard of quality while
reproducing the family recipe
throughout the years, even when
the spread of supermarket chains
between 1960 and 1980 seriously
compromised the production of
unpasteurized cheddar.

When Jamie Montgomery inherited
the role of cheese master within the
family, he spearheaded a revival of
interest in their Cheddar. This led
to an increase in demand amongst
independently run delicatessens
and younger generations, who are
developing the desire to know more
about the foods we eat. Jamie is
committed to overseeing every
stage of the cheese production
on his farm, from the quality of the
grass the cows feed on through to
the taste and texture of the final
product.

LA RUMBERA AREPA WITH ROAST PORK AND GOUDA

Arepa La Rumbera

La Rumbera, which combines slices of tender roast pork and mild Gouda cheese, is one of the most popular arepas in Venezuela. We serve this filling with a choice of sweet red pepper and pork crackling arepas, but feel free to use any of the variations on pages 25–33.

SERVES 12

FOR THE AREPAS

1 quantity of sweet red pepper arepa dough (see page 26)

1 quantity of pork crackling arepa dough (see page 29)

FOR THE BRINE

800 ml (27 fl oz/3¼ cups) water

200 ml (7 fl oz/scant 1 cup) white wine

90 g (3 oz/¼ cup) fine salt

50 g (1¾ oz/¼ cup) sugar

5 garlic cloves

1 tsp thyme leaves

2 bay leaves

FOR THE PORK

3 kg (6 lb 10 oz) pork leg

700 ml (24 fl oz/scant 3 cups) red wine

580 g (1 lb 4 oz/4 cups) roughly chopped carrots

1 kg (2 lb 4 oz/7 cups) roughly chopped onions

580 g (1 lb 4 oz/4 cups) roughly chopped green bell peppers

580 g (1 lb 4 oz/4 cups) roughly chopped celery

TO SERVE

sofrito butter (see page 162)

150 g (5 oz/1¾ cups) grated (shredded) Gouda or yellow cheese

a handful of chopped chives

A day ahead, brine the pork. Place all the ingredients in a bowl and mix until the sugar and salt are dissolved. Submerge the pork in the brine and set aside.

The next day, preheat the oven to 180°C (350°F/Gas 4). Remove the pork from the brine and put it in a deep roasting pan. Add all the remaining ingredients for the pork, cover the pan tightly with foil and cook for 3 hours (or 1 hour for each 1 kg/2 lb of pork). Baste the pork with the cooking juices in the pan every 30 minutes to create a caramelized crust on the meat.

When 40 minutes of cooking time remain, remove the foil so the outer layer of fat on the meat can brown and the flavours deepen.

Following the instructions on pages 26 and 29, shape both of the doughs into 12 arepas and cook them just before serving.

Split open the arepas and scoop out some of their soft insides to make room for the filling. Slice the pork very thinly. Spread the arepas with the sofrito butter and fill them with the slices of pork and grated (shredded) Gouda, then finish with a handful of chopped chives.

Note: Ideally the pork should be brined overnight before roasting, not only for a better taste but also for moisture, avoiding the dryness that often comes with cooking meat.

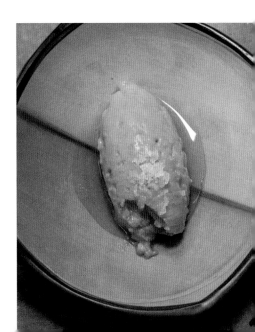

LA PELÚA AREPA WITH PULLED BEEF AND YELLOW CHEESE

Arepa La Pelúa con carne mechada y queso amarillo

SERVES 6

FOR THE AREPAS

1 quantity of basic arepa dough
(see page 18)

FOR THE PULLED BEEF

1 kg (2 lb 4 oz) beef skirt (or veal)

250 g (9 oz/1¼ cups) red sofrito (see
page 159)

80 ml (3 fl oz/⅓ cup) beef broth
(cooking liquid from the beef)

60 ml (2 fl oz/¼ cup) tomato passata

3 tbsp annatto oil

2 tsp English mustard

1 tbsp Worcestershire sauce

1 bay leaf

½ tsp ground cumin

½ tsp black pepper

1 tsp salt

TO SERVE

150 g (5 oz/1 cup) grated (shredded)
yellow cheese

Put the beef skirt in a large pot, cover with water and bring to a boil over a medium heat. Cook for 2 hours, or until the meat is tender and easily shreds. Remove the beef from the pot, reserving the cooking liquid. Pull the meat into shreds using two forks. Cooking 1 kg (2 lb 4 oz) of beef this way should yield approximately 500 g (1 lb 2 oz) of shredded meat.

Once all the beef is pulled, return it to a pan and add all the other ingredients. Cook over a medium heat until the beef is well seasoned and a small amount of liquid is left and the meat is not too dry.

Following the instructions on page 18, shape the dough into 6 arepas and cook them just before serving.

Split open the arepas and scoop out some of their soft insides to make room for the filling. Fill the arepas with the pulled beef and top with the grated (shredded) yellow cheese.

Note: We prefer the pulled beef to be moist with a good amount of gravy. However, if you prefer, cook the beef for longer to dry it out a bit more.

SPIT-ROASTED BEEF AREPA WITH TOMATO AND AVOCADO

Arepa La Llanera, carne en vara con tomate y aguacate

The most iconic dish of the Venezuelan plains, authentic spit-roasted beef (or *carne en vara*) typically has only two additional ingredients: salt and fire. For our version, however, we have added garlic and herbs. The secret to this dish is to slow-cook the beef over a wood fire as it infuses the meat with a specific taste that cannot be achieved using commercially available charcoal.

SERVES 6

FOR THE AREPAS

1 quantity of basic arepa dough (see page 18)

FOR THE SPIT-ROASTED BEEF

1 kg (2 lb 4 oz) picahna (sirloin cap)

salt and pepper, to taste

FOR THE BRINE

1 litre (34 fl oz/4 cups) water

1 garlic clove, halved

1 thyme sprig

10 black peppercorns

1 tbsp coarse salt

TO SERVE

150 g (5 oz/1 cup) grated (shredded) white cheese

heart of palm salsa (*pico de gallo palmito*, see page 164)

1 avocado, finely diced

Following the instructions on page 18, shape the dough into 6 arepas and cook them just before serving.

For the brine, pour the water into a saucepan, add all the other ingredients and bring to a boil. Remove the pan from the heat.

Light the fire at least 40 minutes before cooking.

Season the beef with salt and pepper, then skewer with the wooden spit and cook over the fire for 1 hour (or 1 hour for each 1 kg/2 lb of beef). Baste the beef with the brine every 30 minutes to keep the meat moist.

Check the internal temperature of the meat with a digital probe thermometer. It should be 55–60°C (130–140°F) when ready. When you cut into the meat, the centre should be light brown and the outside should be well cooked and slightly

sink to the touch. At 58°C (136°F) the beef is slightly more than medium rare; you can shorten the cooking time, if preferred. If cooked for any longer, the meat loses its juices and flavour. Leave to rest for 30 minutes before serving.

Split open the arepas and scoop out some of their soft insides to make room for the filling. Slice the beef. Fill the arepas with the slices of beef and grated (shredded) cheese then top with the salsa and diced avocado.

Notes: The wood used for the fire must be very dry. We use guama, guava, or mango tree wood, but use a wood that is native to you and sustainably sourced. However, avoid pine wood, which produces an unpleasant sour aroma.

To be authentically Venezuelan, accompany this arepa with some hot sauce or a good guasacaca, placing a small spoonful on each bite.

ROAST LAMB AREPA WITH CHERRY TOMATOES

Arepa de cordero estofado y tomates cherry asados

SERVES 6

FOR THE AREPAS

1 quantity of basic arepa dough
  (see page 18)

FOR THE LAMB

3 medium white onions

60 g (2 oz) sweet red peppers
  (*ají dulce*)

2 medium red bell peppers

3 large green bell peppers

8 garlic cloves

700 ml (24 fl oz/scant 3 cups)
  red wine

2 tbsp salt

1 tbsp olive oil

2 kg (4 lb 8 oz) leg of lamb

FOR THE GREEN PICADA

2 tbsp rosemary leaves

1 tbsp thyme leaves

1 tsp mint leaves

120 ml (4 fl oz/½ cup) olive oil

FOR THE TOMATOES

200 g (7 oz/1¼ cups) cherry
  tomatoes

2 tbsp olive oil

½ tsp salt

¼ tsp black pepper

1 tsp pepperoncini

2 garlic cloves

A day ahead, make the picada. Combine all the ingredients in a blender and blitz to a smooth paste. Set aside.

Next, marinate the lamb. Finely slice the onion, sweet pepper, red and green peppers and garlic. Combine them in a bowl with all the other ingredients and two-thirds of the picada. Make sure the leg of lamb is fully coated in the marinade. Chill in the fridge for 12 hours.

The next day, preheat the oven to 120°C (250°F/Gas ½). Once the lamb has marinated, place it in a roasting pan and cook in the hot oven for 3 hours, or until the meat comes away from the bone.

Following the instructions on page 18, shape the dough into 6 arepas and cook them just before serving.

Once the lamb is cooked, transfer the meat to a plate and set aside. Using a slotted spoon remove the vegetables from the roasting pan leaving all the meat juices. Skim off any excess fat.

Over a medium heat, reduce the meat juices in the pan, then stir in a generous spoonful of the picada until it is fully incorporated.

Take the lamb off the bone and cut it into thin slices. Cover the slices of lamb with the sauce.

Meanwhile, roast the cherry tomatoes. Slice the tomatoes in half and combine in a bowl with the rest of the ingredients. Spread on a baking tray and bake in the oven at 180°C (350°F/Gas 4), until they start to dehydrate and become golden around the edges. Remove from the oven and set aside.

Split open the arepas and scoop out some of their soft insides to make room for the filling. Fill the arepas with slices of the lamb in the sauce and the roasted tomatoes.

Notes: Instead of roasting the lamb in the oven, you can cook it on a barbecue or grill over hot coals. This will not give you the meat juices needed to make the sauce, however the lamb will be highly flavourful.

ASADO NEGRO AREPA WITH TOMATOES AND AGED CHEESE

Arepa de asado negro, y tomates con queso de año

This dish originated in Caracas during colonial times. Caramelized in a sugar syrup and then cooked in red wine, the beef takes on a near black colour. Each Venezuelan family has their own way of preparing the beef. Some marinate the meat the day before. Some add beer or rum to the sauce. Some vary the vegetables and even add olives.

SERVES 6

FOR THE AREPAS

1 quantity of basic arepa dough (see page 18)

FOR THE ASADO NEGRO (BLACKENED BEEF)

1.5 kg (3 lb 5 oz) beef tenderloin or eye of round

1 tbsp vegetable oil

25 g (1 oz/⅛ cup) granulated sugar

225 g (8 oz/1 cup) finely diced white onion

30 g (1 oz/¼ cup) finely diced red and green sweet peppers (ají dulce, or use sweet red pepper paste)

100 g (3½ oz/¾ cup) finely diced red bell pepper

200 g (7 oz/1½ cups) finely diced green bell pepper

5 garlic cloves

750 ml (25 fl oz/3 cups) red wine

2 bay leaves

salt and pepper, to taste

TO SERVE

150 g (5 oz/1¼ cup) sliced red and yellow cherry tomatoes

150 g (5 oz/1 cup) grated (shredded) aged salty white cheese

Season the beef all over with salt and pepper, then set aside.

Warm the oil in a heavy-based pan or double-walled pot large enough to hold the entire tenderloin. Caramelize the sugar in the oil over a medium heat, but do not let it blacken or cook to the point it smells burnt. If either of these things happen, start again. This first preparation stage is critical for a good asado.

Once you have a dark caramel, add the seasoned beef to the pan and sear it well, turning continuously so it colours evenly. Take care as the caramelized sugar will be very hot.

Remove the seared meat from the pan and add all the vegetables to make a caramelized sofrito. Once the vegetables have been cooking for 10 minutes, add the red wine and bay leaves then return the beef to the pan and cook for 2 hours, or until the meat is tender. Leave to cool.

Following the instructions on page 18, shape the dough into 6 arepas and cook them just before serving.

Cut the beef into slices about 3 cm (1 inch) thick then place the slices back into the sauce to keep warm.

Split open the arepas and scoop out some of their soft insides to make room for the filling. Fill the arepas with slices of the beef in the sauce and the cherry tomatoes, then top with grated (shredded) cheese.

Note: Eye of round is a cut of beef taken from the hind of the animal, usually prepared in Venezuela with sugar, spices, wine and peppers for a dark colour and sweet taste.

HOISIN-GLAZED RIBS AREPA WITH KOREAN SLAW

Arepas de costillas hoisin, ensalada con vinagreta Korean cremosa

SERVES 6

FOR THE AREPAS

1 quantity of basic arepa dough
   (see page 18)

FOR THE MARINADE

3 tbsp vegetable oil

2 tbsp Worcestershire sauce

2 tbsp English mustard

1½ tbsp vinegar

1½ tsp sweet red pepper paste
   (*ají dulce* paste)

1½ tsp onion powder

1½ tsp paprika

1 tsp dried oregano

½ tsp garam masala

1 tsp salt

½ tsp pepper

FOR THE RIBS

600 g (1 lb 5 oz) bone-in pork ribs

150 ml (5 fl oz/scant ⅔ cup)
   hoisin sauce

1 tbsp sesame seeds

½ tbsp chopped chives

FOR THE SLAW

½ medium red cabbage

½ medium white cabbage

1 red onion

2 tbsp finely chopped coriander
   (cilantro)

2 tbsp finely chopped chives

FOR THE VINAIGRETTE

2 medium spring onions (scallions)

10-cm (4-inch) piece of root ginger

2 garlic cloves

2 tbsp Sriracha hot sauce

30 g (1 oz/⅛ cup) granulated sugar

3 tbsp soy sauce

3 tbsp rice vinegar

3 tbsp sesame oil

A day ahead, make the marinade. Combine all ingredients for the marinade and pour over the pork ribs, then leave for 12 hours.

If you have a sous-vide machine at home, place the marinated ribs in a bag, seal and cook for 16 hours at 68°C (154°F). Otherwise, cook the ribs in a 90°C (190°F/Gas ¼) oven for 6 hours. Once cooked, remove the ribs from the bag and set aside. Mix the meat juices left in the bag with the hoisin sauce to make a glaze.

Following the instructions on page 18, shape the dough into 6 arepas and cook them just before serving.

To make the slaw, carefully slice both red and white cabbages and the red onion into evenly sized, thin strips using a mandolin or a very sharp knife.

Rinse the vegetables in cold water with a little vinegar, then drain and combine with the finely chopped herbs in a serving bowl.

To make the vinaigrette, put all the ingredients in a blender and blitz until smooth. Strain through a fine sieve (strainer). Add enough vinaigrette to coat the vegetables to the bowl and toss well.

Sear the cooked pork ribs on the grill, continually brushing them with the hoisin glaze until well caramelized. Scatter the sesame seeds and chives over the glazed ribs.

Split open the arepas and scoop out some of their soft insides to make room for the filling. Fill the arepas with the hoisin-glazed pork ribs and Korean slaw.

Note: Any leftover vinaigrette can be stored in the fridge for up to 2 weeks.

SMOKED CHORIZO AREPA WITH GRILLED VEGETABLES

Arepa de chorizo ahumado, vegetales grillados, mojo criollo

SERVES 6

FOR THE AREPAS

1 quantity of basic arepa dough (see page 18)

FOR THE SAUSAGES

6 smoked chorizo sausages

olive oil, for frying

FOR THE GRILLED VEGETABLES

½ small aubergine (eggplant)
1 medium white onion
3 red or yellow bell peppers

FOR THE DRESSING

2 garlic cloves
25 g (1 oz) thyme leaves
1 tbsp coarse sea salt
80 ml (3 fl oz/⅔ cup) olive oil

TO SERVE

avocado butter (see page 162)
avocado salsa (*guasacaca*, see page 164)
island sauce (*mojo isleño*, see page 164)

Following the instructions on page 18, shape the dough into 6 arepas and cook them just before serving.

Prepare the barbecue or grill at least 40 minutes before cooking.

Cook the chorizo sausages over the coals at a low heat, ensuring they stay juicy and do not dry out. If you cannot cook the sausages over coals, simply cook them in a frying pan (skillet) over a medium heat with a splash of olive oil.

Grill the vegetables over the coals at a low heat until golden. Peel the vegetables, then dice them and combine in a bowl. If you cannot cook the vegetables over coals, simply sauté them in a pan over a medium heat.

To make the dressing, crush the garlic, thyme and salt in a mortar. Gradually add the oil to the garlic mixture. Pour the dressing over the grilled vegetables in the bowl.

Split open the arepas and scoop out some of their soft insides to make room for the filling. Spread the arepas with the avocado butter. Slice the chorizo sausages on the diagonal and lay the slices on the base of each arepa. Fill the arepas with the grilled vegetables then top with the sauces. The sauces can also be served as dips on the side.

REINA PEPIADA AREPA

Arepa La Reina Pepiada

Venezuela became known as a country of beauty queens after Susana Duijm was crowned Miss World in 1955. This popular arepa was christened 'La Reina Pepiada' — or 'The Curvy Queen' — by the Álvarez Brothers at their areperas in Caracas in honour of Susana, the first Venezuelan to win an international beauty contest.

SERVES 6

FOR THE AREPAS

1 quantity of basic arepa dough (see page 18)

FOR THE CHICKEN REINA

300 g (10½ oz/2 cups) poached chicken breast, shredded

300 g (10½ oz/2 cups) finely diced avocado

50 g (1¾ oz/1 cup) fresh peas, cooked in boiling water

30 g (1 oz/⅛ cup) finely diced red onion

30 g (1 oz/¼ cup) finely diced sweet red pepper (*ají dulce*)

30 g (1 oz/¾ cup) chopped coriander (cilantro) leaves

FOR THE MAYONNAISE BASE

1 medium avocado, peeled and pitted

2 garlic cloves, peeled

20 g (¾ oz/½ cup) coriander (cilantro) leaves

1 tsp salt

1 egg yolk

4 tbsp Champagne vinegar or white wine vinegar

1 tbsp Dijon mustard

300 ml (10½ fl oz/1¼ cups) avocado oil

TO SERVE

1 avocado, peeled, pitted and sliced

coarse sea salt and freshly ground black pepper

First, make the mayonnaise base. Put the avocado, garlic, coriander (cilantro) and salt in a blender and blitz until smooth.

Put the egg yolk in a bowl and add the vinegar and mustard. Slowly add the avocado oil in a trickle, whisking continuously, until it emulsifies. Stir in the avocado purée. Set aside until ready to serve.

Following the instructions on page 18, shape the dough into 6 arepas and cook them just before serving.

Make the chicken reina just before serving. Combine all the ingredients in a mixing bowl and add 180 g (6½ oz/1 cup) of the mayonnaise base. Mix well until everything is evenly coated. Cover the bowl with clingfilm (plastic wrap) and chill in the fridge until ready to serve.

Split open the arepas and scoop out some of their soft insides to make room for the filling. Lay the slices of avocado over the base of each arepa and season with salt and pepper, then fill with the chicken reina filling.

Notes: Always prepare the chicken filling with the avocado mayonnaise base just before serving and consume on the same day.

It is best to use white breast meat for this recipe. Poach the chicken breasts in water with onion, celery, carrot and coriander (cilantro) stalks, but you can use other aromatics. Once the chicken breast is cooked, we remove it from the cooking water and shred the meat using two forks and leave it to cool.

Any leftover avocado mayonnaise can be stored in an airtight container in the fridge for later use.

LA SIFRINA AREPA

Arepa La Sifrina

SERVES 6

FOR THE AREPAS

1 quantity of basic arepa dough
(see page 18)

FOR THE CHICKEN REINA

300 g (10½ oz/2 cups) poached
chicken breast, shredded

300 g (10½ oz/2 cups) finely diced
avocado

50 g (1¾ oz/1 cup) fresh peas,
cooked in boiling water

30 g (1 oz/⅛ cup) finely diced
red onion

30 g (1 oz/¼ cup) finely diced sweet
red pepper (*aji dulce*)

30 g (1 oz/¾ cup) chopped coriander
(cilantro) leaves

FOR THE MAYONNAISE BASE

200 g (7 oz/1 cup) mayonnaise

½ avocado, peeled and pitted

40 g (1½ oz/1 cup) coriander
(cilantro) leaves

20 g (¾ oz/¼ cup) finely chopped
white onion

1 tsp Tabasco red pepper sauce

TO SERVE

1 avocado, peeled, pitted and sliced

coarse sea salt and freshly ground
black pepper

150 g (5 oz/1¾ cups) grated
(shredded) Gouda (or other mild
yellow cheese)

First, make the mayonnaise base.
Put all the ingredients in a blender
and blitz until smooth. Set aside.

To make the chicken reina, combine
all the ingredients in a mixing bowl
and add 180 g (6½ oz/1 cup) of the
mayonnaise base. Mix well until
everything is evenly coated. Cover
the bowl with clingfilm (plastic
wrap) and chill in the fridge until
ready to serve.

Following the instructions on page
18, shape the dough into 6 arepas
and cook them just before serving.

Split open the arepas and scoop out
some of their soft insides to make
room for the filling. Lay the slices of
avocado over the base of each
arepa and season with salt and
pepper, then fill with the chicken
reina filling and top with grated
(shredded) Gouda or other mild
yellow cheese.

Note: Always prepare the chicken
filling with the avocado mayonnaise
base just before serving and consume
on the same day.

AREPA LA CATIRA WITH CARACAS-STYLE CHICKEN

Arepa La Catira, pollo Caraqueño y queso Gouda rallado

SERVES 12

FOR THE AREPAS

2 quantities of basic arepa dough
(see page 18)

FOR THE CARACAS-STYLE CHICKEN

450 g (1 lb/2 cups) red sofrito
(see below)

200 g (7 oz/1 cup) sweet red pepper
paste (*ají dulce* paste)

2 tbsp American yellow mustard

2 tbsp Worcestershire sauce

1 bay leaf

2 tsp onion powder

2 tsp ground turmeric

1 tsp smoked paprika

½ tsp annatto seeds

½ tsp ground cumin

240 ml (8 fl oz/1 cup) chicken broth
(from poaching the chicken)

1 kg (2 lb 4 oz/6½ cups) poached
chicken breast, shredded

2 tbsp salt

1 tsp black pepper

FOR THE RED SOFRITO

200 g (7 fl oz/scant 1 cup) annatto oil

650 g (1 lb 7 oz/4¼ cups) diced
white onion

150 g (5 oz/1¼ cups) diced sweet
red pepper (*ají dulce*)

350 g (12 oz/2½ cups) diced red
bell pepper

100 g (3½ oz/½ cup) diced garlic

TO SERVE

avocado butter (see page 162)

150 g (5 oz/1¾ cups) grated
(shredded) Gouda (or other mild
yellow cheese)

First, make the red sofrito. Heat the annatto oil in a heavy-based pan or double-bottomed pot. Add the white onion, sweet red pepper, red bell pepper and garlic then cook over a low-medium heat for 20–30 minutes or until the onion is translucent. It is important to cook the mixture slowly, stirring every 5 minutes with a wooden spoon.

To make the Caracas-style chicken, cook 450 g (1 lb/2 cups) of the red sofrito in a heavy-based pan over a medium heat with the sweet red pepper paste, yellow mustard, Worcestershire sauce, bay leaf, onion powder and other spices.

Pour the chicken broth into the pan and bring to a boil. Add the chicken, season with the salt and pepper, cover and cook for 15 minutes over a medium heat, or until the flavours have mingled. The chicken should be flavourful and juicy.

Following the instructions on page 18, shape the dough into 12 arepas and cook them just before serving.

Split open the arepas and scoop out some of their soft insides to make room for the filling. Spread the arepas with the avocado butter. Fill with the chicken mixture and top with grated (shredded) Gouda or mild yellow cheese.

"When we talk about arepas, we are talking about something sacred, delicious, nurturing, symbolic and mysterious. Like life itself."

Claudio Nazoa, Comedian, Cook and Writer. Caracas.

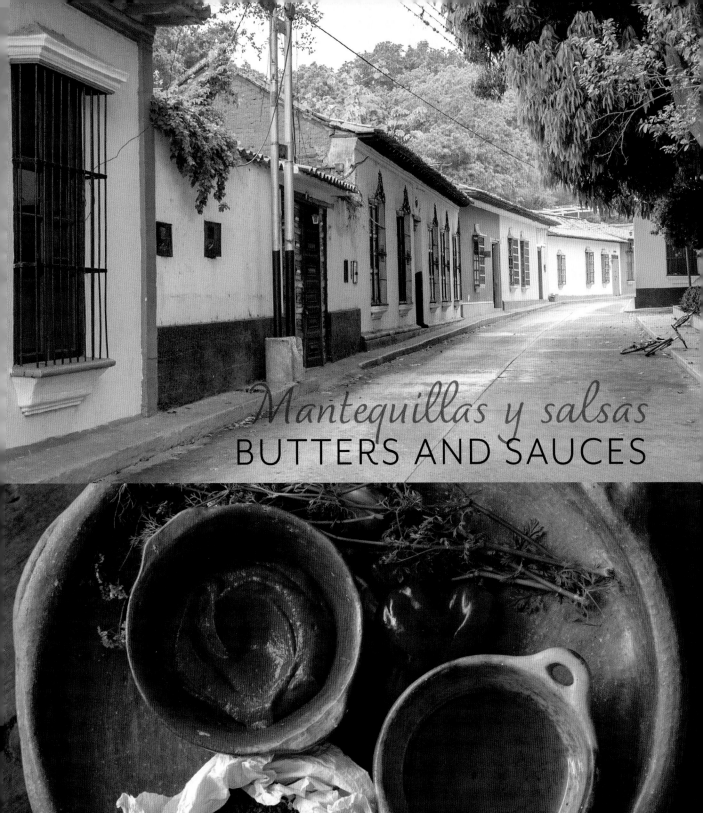

Mantequillas y salsas
BUTTERS AND SAUCES

BUTTERS

Mantequillas

GARLIC AND PARSLEY BUTTER

500 g (1 lb 2 oz/2½ cups) butter
100 g (3½ oz/¾ cup) garlic
100 g (3½ oz/1½ cups) curly parsley
¾ tsp coarse sea salt

Melt the butter in a saucepan over a low-medium heat (do not allow it to brown or caramelize). Roughly chop the garlic. Pick the parsley leaves from the stems and discard the stems. Blanch the leaves in boiling water for 2 seconds, then plunge into iced water. Once the leaves are cold, drain well to remove the water.

Pour the melted butter into a blender, add the chopped garlic, blanched parsley and salt, then blitz well. Strain through a fine sieve (strainer). Store in an airtight container and chill in the fridge until required.

CITRUS BUTTER

500 g (1 lb 2 oz/2½ cups) butter
20 g (¾ oz/3 tbsp) lemongrass
1 tbsp grated (shredded) root ginger
1 tbsp grated (shredded) lemon zest
1 tbsp grated (shredded) lime zest
¾ tsp coarse sea salt

Melt the butter in a saucepan over a low-medium heat (do not allow it to brown or caramelize). Crush the lemongrass in a mortar and add it to the pan. Allow the lemongrass to infuse the butter at a low heat for 10 minutes. Discard the lemongrass.

Pour the melted butter into a blender, add the grated (shredded) ginger, lemon and lime zests and salt, then blitz well. Strain through a fine sieve (strainer). Store in an airtight container and chill in the fridge until required.

SOFRITO BUTTER

500 g (17½ oz/2½ cups) butter
200 g (7 oz/1 cup) red sofrito
  (see page 159)
¾ tsp coarse sea salt

Melt the butter in a saucepan over a low-medium heat (do not allow it to brown or caramelize). Pour the melted butter into a blender, add the sofrito and salt, then blitz well. Strain through a fine sieve (strainer). Store in an airtight container and chill in the fridge until required.

SWEET RED PEPPER BUTTER

500 g (1 lb 2 oz/2½ cups) butter
200 g (7 oz/1 cup) sweet red pepper paste (*ají dulce* paste)
¾ tsp coarse sea salt

Melt the butter in a saucepan over a low-medium heat (do not allow it to brown or caramelize). Pour the melted butter into a blender, add the sweet red pepper paste and salt, then blitz well. Strain through a fine sieve (strainer). Store in an airtight container and chill in the fridge until required.

AVOCADO BUTTER

500 g (1 lb 2 oz/2½ cups) butter
2 medium avocado, peeled and pitted
20 g (¾ oz) red onion
20 g (¾ oz) tomatoes
4 tbsp fresh lime juice
¾ tsp coarse sea salt
¾ tsp black pepper
30 g (1 oz/¼ cup) coriander (cilantro) leaves

Melt the butter in a saucepan over a low-medium heat (do not allow it to brown or caramelize). Pour the melted butter into a blender, add the avocado, red onion, tomato, lime juice, salt, pepper and coriander (cilantro), then blitz well. Strain through a fine sieve (strainer). Store in an airtight container and chill in the fridge until required.

GREEN ONION BUTTER

400 g (14 oz) spring onions (scallions)

500 g (1 lb 2 oz/2½ cups) butter

¾ tsp coarse sea salt

First, char the spring onions (scallions) over an open flame until blackened all over (do not allow them to whiten on the outside). Wrap the charred onions in foil and cook in the oven for 10 minutes at 180°C (360°F/Gas 4), or until soft when pierced with a fork. Remove the charred exterior then finely slice the onions and set aside.

Melt the butter in a saucepan over a low-medium heat (do not allow it to brown or caramelize).

Pour the melted butter into a blender, add the onions and salt, then blitz well. Strain through a fine sieve (strainer). Store in an airtight container and chill in the fridge until required.

TOMATO-ANCHOVY BUTTER

500 g (1 lb 2 oz/2½ cups) butter

100 g (3½ oz/1¾ cups) sundried tomatoes in oil, drained

1 x 50-g (1¾-oz) can of anchovy fillets in oil, drained

Melt the butter in a saucepan over a low-medium heat (do not allow it to brown or caramelize).

Pour the melted butter into a blender, add the tomatoes and anchovies, then blitz well. Strain through a fine sieve (strainer). Store in an airtight container and chill in the fridge until required.

SHRIMP AND SWEET CHILLI PEPPER BUTTER

500 g (1 lb 2 oz/2½ cups) butter

45 prawn (shrimp) heads

100 g (3½ oz/½ cup) sweet red pepper paste (*ají dulce* paste)

¾ tsp coarse sea salt

In a heavy-based pan, sauté the prawn (shrimp) heads with the sweet red pepper paste and salt, lightly crushing the heads.

Melt the butter in a saucepan over a low-medium heat (do not allow it to brown or caramelize). Add the prawns to the melted butter and cook over a low heat for 10 minutes. Remove the prawns, pour the melted butter into a blender and blitz well. Strain through a fine sieve (strainer).

Store in an airtight container and chill in the fridge until required.

RIPE PLANTAIN BUTTER

1 ripe plantain

500 g (1 lb 2 oz/2½ cups) butter

Peel the plantain, brush with a little butter and bake for 40 minutes in a 200°C (400°F) oven until golden. Leave to cool to room temperature.

Melt the butter in a saucepan over a low-medium heat (do not allow it to brown or caramelize).

Pour the melted butter into a blender, add the baked plantain and blitz well. Strain through a fine sieve (strainer). Store in an airtight container and chill in the fridge until required.

SAUCES

Salsas

AVOCADO SALSA (GUASACACA)

This is the Venezuelan version of guacamole, but smoother and made with lots more coriander (cilantro). It is used frequently as a sauce to add flavour to dishes.

250 g (9 oz/1¼ cups) mayonnaise

2 small avocado, peeled and pitted

120 g (4 oz) white onion

100 g (3½ oz) green bell pepper

1 garlic clove

3 tbsp olive oil

3 tbsp white vinegar

1 tbsp salt

2 bunches of coriander (cilantro)

Put all the ingredients in a blender and blitz until smooth. Pass the salsa through a sieve (strainer).

SWEET RED PEPPER AND CORIANDER PURÉE (CHIMICHURRI)

50 ml (1¾ fl oz/¼ cup) vegetable oil

50 g (1¾ oz) sweet red peppers (ají dulce)

1 tbsp apple cider vinegar

10 g (½ oz/⅔ cup) coriander (cilantro) leaves

Heat the oil in a small saucepan over a low heat. Add the sweet red peppers and cook for 20 minutes. Remove the confit peppers from the oil and set aside both to cool to use in the next step.

Once cool, remove the seeds from the confit peppers and blend with the vinegar and coriander (cilantro). Slowly add 35 ml (1¼ fl oz/⅛ cup) of the reserved oil in a trickle until it emulsifies. Season to taste.

HEART OF PALM SALSA (PICO DE GALLO PALMITO)

100 g (3½ oz) heart of palm

50 g (1¾ oz) tomatoes

25 g (¾ oz) white onion

2 tbsp olive oil

1 tbsp white wine vinegar

Finely dice the heart of palm, tomatoes and onion then combine in a bowl with the oil and vinegar. Season with salt to taste.

SPICY WHEY SAUCE (SUERO PICANTE)

250 g (9 oz/2¼ cups) whey

2 tbsp rocoto chilli paste

2 tbsp sweet red pepper paste

Put all the ingredients in a blender and blitz until smooth. Season with salt and pepper to taste.

ISLAND SAUCE (MOJO ISLEÑO)

200 ml (7 fl oz/scant 1 cup) white wine vinegar

4 tbsp each vegetable oil and olive oil

200 g (7 oz) white onion

2 tbsp garlic paste

80 g (2¾ oz/6 cups) coriander (cilantro) leaves

2 tbsp chopped parsley leaves

1 tbsp smoked paprika

Put all the ingredients in a blender and blitz until smooth. Season with salt and pepper to taste.

DESSERTS
Postres

VENEZUELAN-STYLE FLAN

Quesillo

SERVES 6–8

FOR THE FLAN

380 ml (12¾ oz/1⅓ cups minus 1 tbsp) coconut milk

1 x 400-ml (14-oz) can sweetened condensed milk

4 tsp whole (full-fat) milk

4 eggs plus ½ egg yolk

2 tbsp white rum

4 tsp vanilla bean paste

½ tonka bean (optional)

FOR THE CARAMEL

300 g (10½ oz/1½ cups) caster (superfine) sugar, for the caramel

4 tbsp water

To make the flan, preheat the oven to 150°C (300°F/Gas 2). Put the coconut milk, condensed milk, milk, eggs and egg yolk, rum and vanilla bean paste in a blender. Grate in the tonka bean (if using) and blitz until smooth. Pass the mixture through a sieve (strainer) to remove any particles and set aside.

To make the caramel, put the sugar and water in a heavy-based non-stick pan and over a low–medium heat. Do not stir as this can cause the sugar to crystallize. Once the sugar starts to dissolve, increase the heat to medium–high and watch the caramel until it turns a dark amber colour. As soon as the caramel darkens in colour, immediately remove the pan from the heat to avoid burning the caramel. If the caramel does burn, discard the contents of the pan and start again.

Carefully pour the hot caramel into a 20-cm (8-inch) flan mould with a lid. (If you do not have a flan mould with a lid, you can use a regular cake pan and tightly cover it with foil.) Tilt the mould or pan to evenly coat the base and sides with the caramel. Leave it to rest for a few minutes to allow the caramel to harden.

Pour the flan mixture into the mould or pan to cover the caramel layer. Sharply tap the mould or pan on the countertop to disperse any air bubbles in the flan mixture. Cover with the lid or foil.

Place the flan mould or cake pan in a deep roasting pan and pour in enough hot water so that it comes three-quarters of the way up the sides of the mould or pan. Place the pan in the hot oven and bake the flan for 2–2¼ hours. Periodically check there is enough water in the roasting pan and top up as needed.

Once the flan is just set, remove from the oven and leave to cool to room temperature. Once the flan is cool, chill in the fridge for 24 hours.

To release the flan from the mould, remove the lid or foil and shake it gently until it comes away from the sides. If necessary, slide a knife around the edges to loosen the flan. Invert the flan onto a serving plate and remove the mould or pan. Slice the flan into individual portions, in the size and shape preferred and spoon over any caramel.

Note: To decorate the flan with sugar swirls, make a second batch of caramel. As soon as it turns golden, drizzle spoonfuls of the hot caramel onto parchment paper in any shape you like. Leave the caramel decorations to harden, then nestle them into the tops of the flan.

COCONUT RICE PUDDING

Arroz con leche

SERVES 6–8

960 ml (32 fl oz/4 cups) coconut
    milk

200 g (7 oz/1 cup) long-grain
    white rice

2 cinnamon sticks

8 cloves

grated (shredded) zest of ⅛ orange

grated (shredded) zest of ½ lime

480 ml (16¼ oz/2 cups) oat milk

220 g (7¾ oz/1 cup) granulated sugar

60 g (2 oz/½ cup) cornflour
    (corn starch)

ground cinnamon, to taste

edible flowers, to decorate

Put the coconut milk, rice, cinnamon sticks, cloves, orange zest and lime zest in a saucepan over a very low heat and cook for 1 hour, or until the milk has reduced by one-quarter to one-third according to your preferred thickness.

Mix half of the oat milk with the sugar, and add to the reduced coconut rice. Cook for a further 15 minutes, stirring continuously.

Pour the remaining oat milk into a blender, add the cornflour (corn starch) and blitz together until smooth. Add this mixture to the pan with the warm coconut rice.

Heat everything for a few more minutes until the rice pudding thickens further. Remember that the rice pudding will continue to thicken some more as it cools.

Pour the coconut rice pudding into a large bowl and leave to cool and set. Once cool, chill the rice pudding in the fridge.

To serve, spoon the coconut rice pudding into individual bowls. Sprinkle with ground cinnamon to taste and decorate with edible flowers (if using).

Note: You may add more or less coconut milk to achieve your preferred taste and consistency.

CHURROS WITH CHOCOLATE SAUCE

Churros y salsa de chocolate

Churros are Spanish in origin, but they are one of those desserts that are loved the world over. The churros at our restaurant, Alma Cocina Latina, are a big hit and so we are sharing the recipe with you. The highlight here is the chocolate sauce, which is made with Herencia Divina Venezuelan Chocolate with 60% cocoa solids. Of course, feel free to use any other high-quality chocolate you prefer.

FOR THE CHURROS

180 ml (6 fl oz/¾ cup) sparkling water

150 ml (5 fl oz/scant ⅔ cup) whole (full-fat) milk

2 tbsp double (heavy) cream

80 g (2¾ oz/⅓ cup) unsalted butter

1 heaped tbsp caster (superfine) sugar

1 tsp fine salt

200 g (7 oz/1½ cups) plain (all-purpose) flour

1 large or extra large egg (at room temperature)

canola oil, for deep-frying

caster (superfine) sugar and ground cinnamon, for dusting

FOR THE CHOCOLATE SAUCE

200 g (7 oz/1½ cup) good-quality chocolate (at least 60% cocoa solids), broken into pieces

300 ml (10½ fl oz/1¼ cups) double (heavy) cream

100 ml (3½ fl oz/scant ½ cup) half-and-half (or use a mixture of double/heavy cream and whole/full-fat milk)

50 g (1¾ oz/¼ cup) butter

3 tbsp liquid glucose

4 tbsp sweetened condensed milk

First, make the chocolate sauce. Put the chocolate in a heatproof bowl and melt it over a bain marie or in a microwave. Set aside.

Put all the other ingredients except the sweetened condensed milk in a pan and heat until blended, stirring continuously.

Remove the pan from the heat and add the melted chocolate and sweetened condensed milk. Stir again until everything is well blended and the sauce is smooth. Pour the chocolate sauce into an airtight container and set aside until ready to serve.

When you're ready to make the churros, weigh out each ingredient before you begin.

Combine the sugar and ground cinnamon for dusting in a bowl.

Pour the sparkling water, milk and double (heavy) cream into a saucepan. Add the butter, sugar and salt to the pan and place over a medium-high heat until the mixture comes to a low boil. Quickly but carefully add the flour to the pan and mix vigorously with a spatula until the mixture is smooth, firm, and dark yellow in colour.

Immediately take the pan off the heat and transfer the mixture to the bowl of an electric mixer. Mix at a low speed for 5 minutes to lower the temperature of the dough and allow the gluten to form.

Add the egg and mix until it is fully incorporated.

Meanwhile, fill a large heavy-based pan with the canola oil and heat to 175–190°C (350–375°F).

Fit a piping (pastry) bag with a wide star-shaped nozzle (tip) and fill the bag with the warm dough. To shape one churro, squeeze out a 20-cm (8-inch) length of the dough and carefully lower it into the hot oil, without splashing.

Keep the churro moving in the oil while it is frying to ensure it browns evenly. Once the churro is golden brown all over, remove it from the oil with a slotted spoon or skimmer and place on a baking sheet. Dust each churro with the cinnamon sugar as soon you take it out of the pan.

Working in batches, continue to fry the churros until all the dough has been used. If there is any dough left over, pipe extra churros onto a baking sheet, silicone sheet or parchment paper and store in the freezer ready for deep-frying at a later date.

Serve the hot churros immediately with the warm chocolate sauce.

CORN CAKE

Torta de jojoto

SERVES 8

FOR THE CORN CAKE

400 g (14 oz/2 cups) sweet yellow corn (cooked kernels)

150 ml (5 fl oz/scant ⅔ cup) double (heavy) cream

75 g (2½ oz/scant ¾ cup) plain (all-purpose) flour, sifted

150 g (5 oz/⅔ cup) caster (superfine) sugar

75 g (2⅔ oz) Cotija cheese (aged salty cows' milk cheese)

1 tsp baking powder

1 tsp fine salt

3 extra large eggs

100 g (3½ oz/½ cup) butter, melted and cooled to room temperature

TO SERVE

white cheese, grilled and crumbled (optional)

sugar cane syrup (*melao*, see page 33, optional)

Preheat the oven to 150°C (300°F/Gas 2). Grease a 23-cm (9-inch) round cake pan and line it with parchment paper.

Put the corn kernels and cream in a blender and blend well.

In a large mixing bowl, combine the flour, sugar, Cotija cheese, baking powder and salt.

Separate the egg whites from the yolks. Set aside the yolks for use later. In a mixing bowl, beat the egg whites with a metal whisk until they are thick and fluffy.

Add the blended corn mixture to the flour and mix with the beater. Add the melted butter and egg yolks. Continue to mix until everything is fully incorporated.

Fold the beaten egg whites into the mixture with a silicone spatula.

Pour the cake mixture into the prepared cake pan. Bake in the hot oven for 50 minutes, or until the tip of a knife inserted into the centre comes out clean with no crumbs.

Leave the cake to cool on a wire rack before turning it out of the pan. Slice into individual portions in the size and shape preferred. Serve the cake with the crumbled white cheese scattered over the top. The cheese can be grilled before being crumbled, if preferred. Drizzle over a few drops of sugar cane syrup (*melao*), if using.

COCKTAILS
Cocteles

TRADITIONAL COCKTAILS AND BEVERAGES

Cocteles y bebidas tradicionales

In a book dedicated to arepas, how could we not include a few favourite cocktails made from Venezuelan rum, one of the greatest gifts from our land. Native rums are at the core of our cocktails, since the local sugar cane provides this exceptional spirit. The sun, rain and wind come together in our tropical climate to create favourable weather conditions for growing sugar cane, from which rum is made. The Venezuelan fields are the birthplace of many agricultural and industrial processes that have helped local rums attain a very high quality, leading them to receive worldwide acclaim. Venezuelan rums have unique qualities that distinguish them from all others and are considered to be some of the best rums in the world.

Venezuelan law rigorously regulates, among other things, the process of aging rum in oak casks. Local law dictates that the label of each bottle must clearly state how long the rum has been aged, indicating the age of the youngest rum used in the blend. Venezuelan rum must be aged for no less than two years. This legal regulation does not apply to rums made with only one type of rum, or 'single cask' rums.

In 2003, Venezuelan rums were internationally recognized and awarded *Denominazione di origine controllata* (DOC) status. This means that any rum labelled as Venezuelan must not only be produced in the geographic regions of Venezuela but they must also meet the high standards that this designated status requires, including a two-year aging period in white oak casks and an anhydrous alcohol content of 40%.

I have also included a recipe for a cocktail that showcases a very new and exceptional Venezuelan spirit made with rainforest ingredients, José Gregorio Ancestral Liqueur. This spirit is not yet readily available worldwide, but it is growing in popularity and promotes some of the previously unfamiliar species of vegetation of the rainforest. And for hot days and those not interested in imbibing, I offer recipes for two non-alcoholic drinks that are dear to all Venezuelans.

"In the poetic imagination of those of us who are cultivators of rum lives a sensation of magical history that is activated every time our lips are wet with its graces. They are stories of the colony, black and white legends, stories of raised and submissive slaves, the independence epic, lost lands and recovered lands, the music that accompanies it to the sound of the drum, its aphrodisiac properties and in general as a remedy for the soul, because it is a medicine against depression."

Humberto Márquez, Journalist.

PAPA HEMINGWAY

Papa Hemingway

SERVES 1

45 ml (1½ oz) Santa Teresa Claro Rum

30 ml (1 oz) Giffard Crème de Pamplemousse Rose Liqueur

7 ml (¼ oz) Strega Liqueur

15 ml (½ oz) fresh lemon juice

7 ml (¼ oz) fresh lime juice

1 dash grapefruit bitters

dried grapefruit slice, to garnish

Combine all the ingredients in a cocktail shaker filled with ice and shake vigorously for 15–20 seconds or until the shaker is frosted on the outside.

Strain into an old fashioned glass or rocks glass filled with a rock of ice. Garnish with a dried grapefruit slice.

VIEJO PIRATA

Viejo pirata

SERVES 1

22 ml (¾ oz) Plantation Stiggins Fancy Pineapple Rum

22 ml (¾ oz) Rittenhouse Straight Rye

15 ml (½ oz) Luxardo

15 ml (½ oz) sweet vermouth

2 dashes Bittermens Xocolatl Mole Bitters

2 dashes Angostura aromatic bitters

avocado leaf, to garnish

Combine all the ingredients in a mixing glass and stir for 30 seconds. Strain into a goblet filled with a rock of ice. Garnish with an avocado leaf.

COFFEE OLD FASHIONED

Pasado de moda

SERVES 1

60 ml (2 fl oz) Pampero Aniversario
   Rum

15 ml (½ fl oz) Venezuelan coffee syrup
   (see below)

2 dashes Bittermens Elemakule
   Tiki Bitters

dried grapefruit slice, to garnish

FOR THE COFFEE SYRUP

250 g (9 oz/2 cups) finely ground
   Venezuelan coffee beans

960 ml (32 fl oz/4 cups) water

900 g (32 oz/4 cups) caster
   (superfine) sugar

First, make the coffee syrup. Put the
coffee in a pot, add the water and
bring to a boil. Stir in the sugar until
dissolved, lower the heat and reduce
the syrup for 10 minutes. Remove
from the heat and strain the syrup
through a coffee filter. Leave to cool.

To mix the cocktail, combine the rum,
coffee syrup and bitters in mixing glass
filled with ice and stir for 30 seconds.

Strain into a rocks glass filled with a
rock of ice. Garnish with a dried
grapefruit slice.

Note: This recipe yields more coffee
syrup than needed to make one
cocktail. Any leftover syrup can be
stored in an airtight container or sealed
bottle to use later.

ANCESTRAL SPIRIT

Espíritu Ancestral

José Gregorio is a medium-sweet liqueur made of two primary botanicals: copoazú (*Theobroma grandiflorum*), a fruit native to the rainforest that some say is the grandfather of cacao, and elderflowers from the elder tree (*Sambucus nigris*), commonly used to make cordial. The result is a sour-and-sweet flavour that is difficult to describe, but is reminiscent of cacao mucilage (the white flesh around the cacao bean inside the pod) with a fruity and flowery aroma.

Named after José Gregorio, the highly renowned Venezuelan physician (1864–1919) to whom many miracles were attributed, the recipe for this liqueur was created on April 30th, 2021, the same day that Gregorio was beatified by the Roman Catholic Church.

SERVES 1

60 ml (2 fl oz) José Gregorio Ancestral Liqueur

30 ml (1 oz) fresh lime juice (or rainforest *limon-mandarina* juice)

15 ml (½ fl oz) simple sugar syrup

15 ml (½ fl oz) pasteurized egg white (from a carton)

3 dashes Angostura aromatic bitters

edible flowers, to garnish

Combine all the ingredients in a cocktail shaker filled with ice and shake vigorously for 15–20 seconds or until the shaker is frosted on the outside. Strain the cocktail into a mixing glass and discard the ice.

Return the cocktail to the shaker and dry shake without ice to emulsify the egg white. Strain into a coupe glass. Garnish with edible flowers.

PASSION FRUIT FIZZ

Coctel de la pasión

SERVES 1

60 ml (2 fl oz) Santa Teresa 1796 Rum

15 ml (½ fl oz) fresh lime juice

30 ml (1 fl oz) passion fruit syrup (see below)

90 ml (3 fl oz) club soda

1 lime wheel, to garnish

1 mint sprig, to garnish

FOR THE PASSION FRUIT SYRUP

240 ml (8 fl oz/1 cup) passion fruit pulp (from a carton or frozen)

960 ml (32 fl oz/4 cups) water

10 whole allspice pods

750 g (1 lb 10 oz/3⅓ cups) demerara sugar or unrefined raw cane sugar

First, make the passion fruit syrup. Put the passion fruit pulp and 240 ml (8 fl oz/1 cup) of the water into a blender and blitz to a smooth purée. Set aside.

Put 720 ml (24 fl oz/3 cups) of the water into a pot, add the allspice pods and bring to a boil. Once boiling, stir in the sugar until dissolved. Lower the heat and reduce the syrup for 10 minutes. Remove from the heat and leave to cool.

Add the passion fruit purée to the cooled syrup, then strain through a fine sieve (strainer).

To mix the cocktail, combine the rum, lime juice, passion fruit syrup and club soda in a mixing glass filled with ice and stir for 30 seconds. Strain into a highball or collins glass filled with ice. Garnish with a lime wheel and mint sprig.

Note: This recipe makes more passion fruit syrup than needed to make one cocktail. Any leftover syrup can be stored in the fridge in an airtight container or sealed bottle.

PAPELÓN WITH LIME

Papelón con limón

In Venezuela's tropical climate, this drink provides much-needed refreshment. A popular limeade, *Papelón con limón* is served daily in cafés, arepa bars and roadside stands.

SERVES 6

240 ml (8 fl oz/1 cup) sugar syrup (see below)

210 ml (7 fl oz/scant 1 cup) fresh lime juice

600 ml (20 fl oz/2½ cups) water

lemon and lime wheels, to garnish

FOR THE SUGAR SYRUP

500 g (1 lb 2 oz/2⅔ cups) unrefined raw cane sugar (such as *papelón*, *panela* or *piloncillo*)

240 ml (8 fl oz/1 cup) water

First, make the sugar syrup. Put the raw cane sugar into a pan, add the water and warm over a medium-high heat for 15 minutes, stirring, until you have a thick syrup. Remove from the heat and leave to cool.

To mix the drink, combine the syrup, lime juice and water in a jug (pitcher), fill with ice and stir for 30 seconds. Adjust the sweetness to taste.

Pour into a collins glass filled with ice. Garnish with lemon and lime wheels. Serve cold.

Note: This recipe makes more sugar syrup than needed to make a serving for six people. Any leftover syrup can be stored in an airtight container or sealed bottle to use later.

COCADA

Cocada

When I was young, my mother would drive us from Caracas to the beach each weekend. The first stop was always a roadside stand in La Guaira for a refreshing coconut drink, traditional in coastal areas. It is so loved there are now stands in many regions, especially where it's hot.

SERVES 6

300 ml (10 fl oz/1¼ cups) coconut water

100 g (3½ oz/1¼ cups) grated (shredded) coconut meat (you can use fresh or frozen)

150 ml (5 fl oz/⅔ cup) coconut milk

130 g (4½ oz/½ cup) sweetened condensed milk

1 tsp ground cinnamon (optional)

Put the coconut water and coconut meat in a blender and blitz until smooth. With the motor running, slowly pour in the coconut milk in a continuous thread until fully incorporated and smooth.

Add the sweetened condensed milk to the coconut drink. Check the sweetness and adjust to your preference. Stir in the ground cinnamon to taste, if using.

Pour into a collins glass filled with crushed ice and stir well to mix. Serve cold.

SOURCING INGREDIENTS

Ají amarillo: A yellow chilli pepper with a fruity flavour. Recipes often call for them in the form of a paste, which can be store-bought.

Ají chirel: A small chilli pepper that is very hot. They can be green, orange or red depending on their degree of ripeness.

Ají dulce: A sweet red chilli pepper with a mild flavour. Recipes frequently call for them either raw or as a paste, which can be store-bought.

Annatto: The seeds of the annatto tree (*Bixa orellana*) have a nutty flavour. They can be ground into a powder or infused into an oil.

Cassava/casabe: Casabe is a traditional Venezuelan crispy, thin flatbread. It is made with flour gained from cassava, an ancient plant (*Manihot esculenta*) native to the northern parts of South America.

Chicharrón: Fried pork rind or crackling skin.

Chocolate: Venezuela produces some of the world's best cacao and chocolate. We use artisanal brand Chocolateria Herencia Divina. instagram.com/chocolateria_hd

Harina P.A.N. maize flour (cornmeal): Pre-cooked maize flour (cornmeal) that is used for all our arepa recipes. It is made from dried, cooked corn kernels that are then finely ground. Harina P.A.N. is popular across Venezuela and our preferred brand. This flour must not be confused with corn flour in the UK or cornstarch in the US.

José Gregorio Ancestral Liqueur: A medium-sweet liqueur that is both fruity and floral, produced by Ancestral Destileria Artesanal. instagram.com/destilerosancestrales

Kumache sauce and salt: An unusual hot sauce or salt made from rainforest chillis and red ants. Kumache has a very specific flavour that cannot be replicated.

Lemon ants: Edible, lemony tasting, non-stinging ants found in the rainforest.

Nata: A sweeter Latin sour cream. Make your own by combining double (heavy) cream, lemon and salt.

Panela/papelón/pilconcillo: Unrefined raw cane sugar with a complex caramel flavour that is made by reducing sugarcane juice.

Plantains: Often called green bananas, they are larger and starchier than yellow bananas. They can be used ripe (black) or unripe (green).

Queso: Venezuelan cheeses are now exported across the world. If you can't source a specific cheese, most can be substituted by *queso fresco* (a mild, crumbly cheese similar to paneer), *queso Cotija* (an aged, salty cows' milk cheese) or *queso Oaxaca* (a semi-hard cows' milk cheese similar to mozzarella). Alternatively, look for Mexican cheeses in Latin American markets. instagram.com/sabanerocheese

Rainforest ingredients: Buying ingredients like lemon ants, kumache and tonka beans directly from Sabores Aborígenes Venezolanos you are supporting sustainable sources of revenue for indigenous communities of Southern Venezuela, which serve as income alternatives to gold mining. instagram.com/saborigenes

Tonka beans: The seeds of the kumaru tree. Their fruity, floral, spicy aroma is reminiscent of vanilla and cinnamon. They are mainly infused into milk, cream and custard.

INDEX

ACKNOWLEDGMENTS

This book was born in our restaurant, Alma Cocina Latina, Baltimore. While we were discussing an arepa menu, I started researching (out of curiosity) what had been written on the subject. I was surprised there were only the odd recipe and article here and there, but no comprehensive book on this very important part of our gastronomy; the one food the Venezuelan population eats on a daily basis. I was inspired to create the first thorough arepa cookbook in English, for the world to enjoy.

Making a book takes a village, a team, a strong family, all of whom must trust in each other. I am deeply grateful to every person who has helped along the way, even in the smallest way.

Joseph Fragoso and Empresas Polar, the first supporters and sponsor of this project. Leda Scheintaub, for helping to write the proposal for this book. Ivanova Decán Gambus, for her invaluable stories about and historic references to Venezuelan gastronomy, and for being my 'Ladilla' sister. Diana Boccardo, for her presence and translation at the start of this all. Diana Rangel Lampe, for her artistic sensibility in visually editing the book concept with the aesthetic that it merits. Claudio Nazoa, for being the funniest 'bodyguard' ever while we photographed the Caracas markets, using his popularity to open doors that would have otherwise remained closed. Carolina Sotillo, for being my fearless companion and driver in Caracas, getting us safely through unsafe places so I could take the photographs, some that you see here. Annie and Alfredo Rangel Lampe, for their contagious laughter and letting us use their home as the stage for all the arepa-related photographs in this book and for graciously providing all the gorgeous props. Gabriela Gamboa, the translator of most texts and recipes in this book, always present when needed despite a crazy schedule. Virginia Allen, open day and night to help keep us sane, and also contributor to making this book an easy reading for an international audience. Marisa Dobson, for helping me navigate the publishing world. Argenis Ramirez, sharing his entire process for making an Arepa Pelá. Santa Teresa rum, for its superb quality, the audacious community programs they develop and their generous support towards the making of this book. Tara Sheperd, our fabulous PR, spreading the word of everything we do at Alma. Pedro Luis (Peyoyo) Rafalli for sharing his passion and knowledge of our rums. Elisa Murillo, talented muralist whose work adorns Alma Cocina Latina's walls, and created the map that you find in the book. Hilton Carter, plant guru extraordinaire, who kindly introduced me to RPS and CICO Books and who quickly became an important friend in our lives, along with his wife Fiona.

Lisa Pendreigh, our editor, whose remarkable patience has been much appreciated. Leslie Harrington, Geoff Borin and Julia Charles, creative director, designer and editor respectively who took on the story of the arepa and its spread around the world!

To my family. My parents for teaching me to look at life attentively, to enjoy its beauty and myriad expressions, and to give back the best way I can. Eduardo and Rosy Stein, for taking me everywhere in Venezuela to provide most of the photographs in this book. Axel and André Stein, for their brotherly enthusiasm, always checking in on my wellbeing and quickly responding to my needs while making this book. Sofia de Ramel, for being my best work of art. My grand-children, Ezra, Elliot, and Eloise for always telling me what's cool and what's not, and for carrying my DNA. Not a simple matter. And finally, my life companion and husband Mark Demshak who has helped every step of the way with abundant smiles, jokes (good and bad), patience, and love; and his children Drew, Franny, and Emmy for always rooting for me. Close friends, always attentive to the pulse of this book while it grew: Daniel and Betty Chemers, Rita Costa Gomes, Régis de Ramel, Amy Karlen, D. Watkins, Kondwani Fidel, Devin Allen, Jessica Agulló, John Shields, Jose Ignacio (Nacho) Useche, Charisse Nichols.

To the chefs and their kitchen team. Eduardo Egui, chef in Venezuela and Spain, the author of all arepa recipes in this book, who presents to us their infinite possibilities and makes them as beautiful as they can be. Always attentive to the thousand and one questions. And meeting me three times in Venezuela to photograph and test the recipes under the warm, tropical light. Always with love, steadiness and calm. And now, I thank him for his friendship. His lovely team:

Laida Yeni Suárez, Yaneidi Yakelin Suárez, Miguel Angel Zambrano, Johan Monzón, Rosa Alvarado, Dayana Martinez, Reiner Perez and Roosevelt Hidalgo.

David Zamudio, Executive Chef and Partner at Alma Cocina Latina, who joins the book via appetizer and dessert recipes, with his sharp dedication to deliciousness. His plates, beautiful and incredibly good, always bring a smile to those who visit his flavours surrounded by the Alma garden. Our dedicated Alma team: Aaron Joseph, Alex Higdon, Maja Griffin for their popular cocktails throughout Alma's years. Maria Alejandra Cobarrubia, pastry chef, and all our behind-the-scenes essential contributors: Nicolas Peña, Kanae Hashimoto, Maritza Arriaza, Carolina Escalante, Edin Aguilar, Omar Torres, Josias Iglesias, Emilio Oliva and Blanca Flores, Luis Ochoa and Emilio Oliva.

ABOUT THE AUTHORS

IRENA STEIN is a photographer, restaurateur, immigrant, sustainability advocate, and humanitarian. Irena came to the United States from Venezuela on a Fulbright Scholarship to Stanford University where she graduated with a Master's in Cultural Anthropology. Since then, she has merged her passion for art, food, community, and environmentalism into a seamless blend in a city that craved it—Baltimore, Maryland. Irena was the first to bring contemporary and highly imaginative Venezuelan cuisine to the United States at her restaurant Alma Cocina Latina. Alma continues to lead the Baltimore food scene with innovative and transformative ideas, not only with their cuisine, but in shaping how we view food in our society. Irena lives in Baltimore, Maryland with her husband and continues to build meaningful cultural connections in the Baltimore area and beyond.

EDUARDO EGUI is a Venezuelan chef with over 20 years experience in the industry. His career includes a number of high-end kitchens like Restaurante Malabar under chef Carlos García. He also worked for García as a member of the opening team at Alto, and in Spain with Andoni Luis